Lord Have Mercy

St Gargoyle's cartoons have appeared regularly in the *Church Times* since 1994 as well as in a series of calendars and in *A Year at St Gargoyle's* published by the Canterbury Press.

Their creator, 'Ron' is a parish priest in deepest Dorset and, he claims, each one is based on something that really happened to someone in a church somewhere. . . .

Also available in the St Gargoyle's range

A Year at St Gargoyle's

The original collection of cartoons following the antics of clergy, choir and congregation through the Church year.

1–85311–315–8 128pp £4.99

St Gargoyle's Postcards

Enliven your social correspondence with this pack of eight assorted correspondence cards, featuring all-time favourite cartoons.

1–85311–357–3 Pack of 8 £2.49

St Gargoyle's Calendar

Enjoy twelve months of parish eccentricity and organize your life – all for £4.25!

Published in May each year.

Prices include VAT, postage and packing

To order: fax your credit card details to 01603-624483 or send a cheque payable to SCM – Canterbury Press Ltd to:

SCM – Canterbury Press Ltd
St Mary's Works
St Mary's Plain
Norwich NR3 3BH

Lord Have Mercy

It's another year at St Gargoyle's!

Ron

CANTERBURY
PRESS
Norwich

Text and illustrations © Ron 2001

First published 2001 by The Canterbury Press Norwich
(a publishing imprint of Hymns Ancient & Modern Limited,
a registered charity)
St Mary's Works, St Mary's Plain,
Norwich, Norfolk NR3 3BH

British Library Cataloguing in Publication Data

A catalogue record for this book is available
from the British Library

ISBN 1–85311–410–3

Typeset by Rowland Phototypesetting Ltd,
Bury St Edmunds, Suffolk and
printed in Great Britain by
St Edmundsbury Press Ltd,
Bury St Edmunds, Suffolk

Foreword

Those of you familiar with the annual cartoon books of the late great cartoonist Giles will remember the 'forewords', usually written for him by the great and the good. Occasionally, however, he had to resort to asking members of his family to oblige, and so it is this year with Ron. The vicar's slush fund obviously being a bit on the low side, he has asked me (big sister) to do the honours. Who better to fill you in on his dark side, to 'out' him for being a closet Meccano addict?

As far back as I can remember, Ron has wanted to be an artist – when we were little we thought artists were people who did not go outside the lines when colouring in. We used to ask our poor parents to judge which of us had produced the better picture; what an exercise in tact and diplomacy that was for them! We were children who drew and painted on anything we could lay our hands on, the insides of Christmas cards, the white paper from the butcher that did not have too much blood on it, you name it we used it. We cut and stuck long before Blue Peter made it fashionable, but Ron always had the edge on me. While I embraced sewing and craft work, he continued with pencil and paint. The talent for cartoons started in his teens; he would do them for my schoolfriends (for a modest fee), and had his first in print in the *Daily Mirror*. Always he had a strong affinity with the absurd, which clearly helps him in his pastoral life today. It must be something to do with all those radio programmes we loved: *The Goons*, *The Navy Lark*, and best of all, *Round the Horn* (I'm giving our ages away now). Our church always knew who to ask when they wanted something daft organising, like the dwile flonking at the summer fete.

Ron was also the family rebel; the rows there were with Dad over long hair, flower-power shirts, Chelsea boots, guitar practice, loud music – especially the music! How proud he would have been of him today.

As you browse through this set of cartoons, I know there will be many chords struck, as parish life is often even funnier than Ron shows. As you recognize people from your own congregations, or, dare I say it – yourselves, have a good look at the church buildings as most of them are taken from life too. We his family also have to watch out, we never know when a character will look horribly familiar.

We never expected Ron to become a priest, but like everything else he does he is good at it. I mentioned the loud music before; his all time favourite group was, and still is, the Byrds. From the words of their greatest hit I give you a text which has clearly influenced him; it is from Ecclesiastes chapter 3: 'To everything there is a season, and a time to every purpose under the heaven . . . a time to laugh.'

Thanks Ron.

Lesley Cobb
January 2001

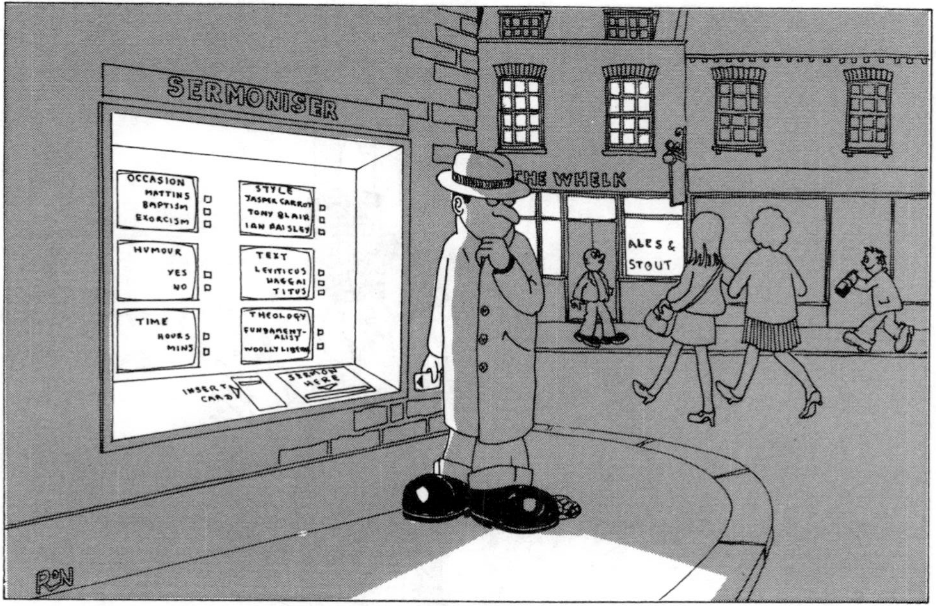
SERMONISER
OCCASION
MATTINS
BAPTISM
EXORCISM
STYLE
JASPER CARROT
TONY BLAIR
IAN PAISLEY
HUMOUR
YES
NO
TEXT
LEVITICUS
HAGGAI
TITUS
TIME
HOURS
MINS
THEOLOGY
FUNDAMENT-ALIST
WOOLLY
INSERT CARD
SERMON HERE
HE WHELK
ALES & STOUT
RON

Desperate beyond measure, late Saturday night, Trevor visited the hole in the wall . . .

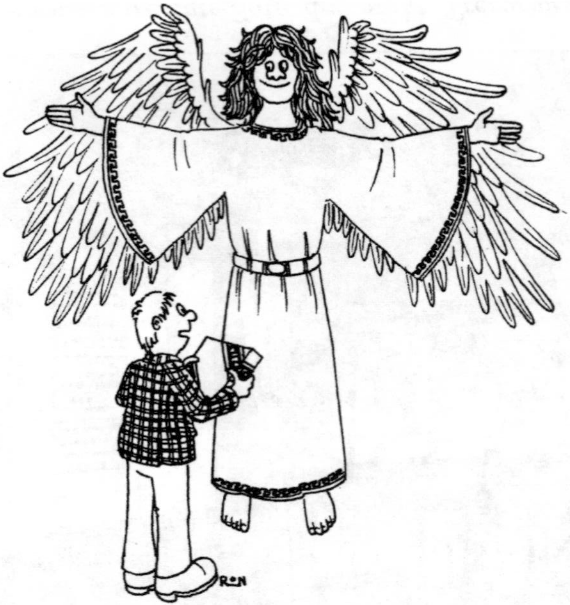
RON

'But I ordered deep pan', protested Trevor, 'and this is thin and crispy!'

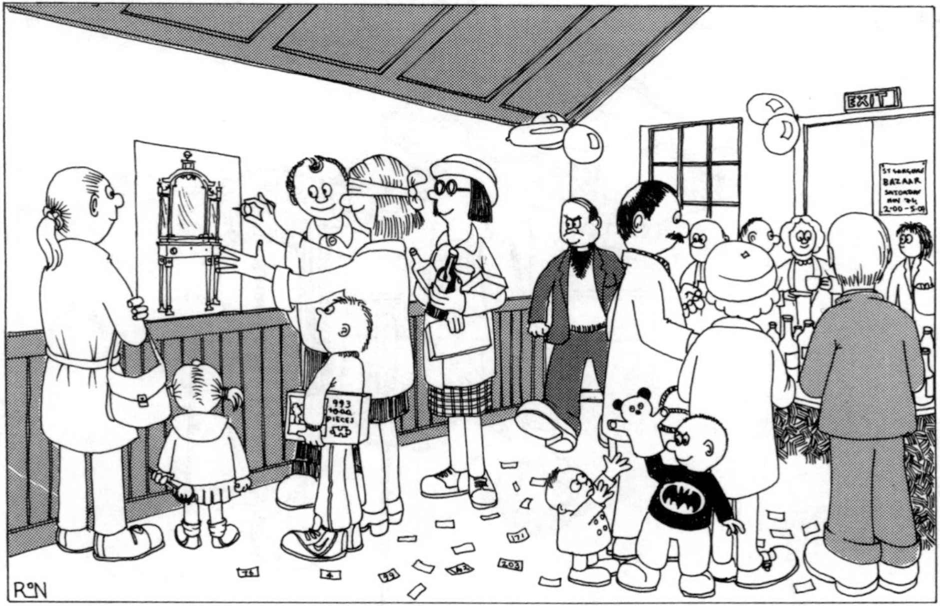
EXIT
BAZAAR

A popular item at the Bazaar was 'Pinning the knob on the Chippendale'.

THE ECHO
SUN
RON DREW THIS - WORLD EXCLUSIVE!

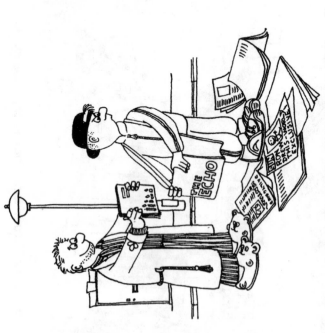

The Revd Henry Snipweed couldn't wait for his copy of What Candle Monthly.

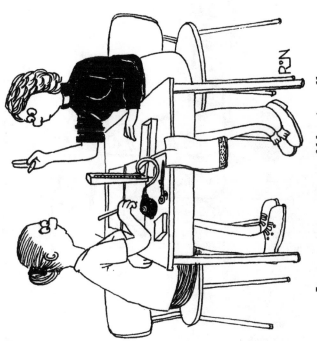

It was a severe case of blessing elbow.

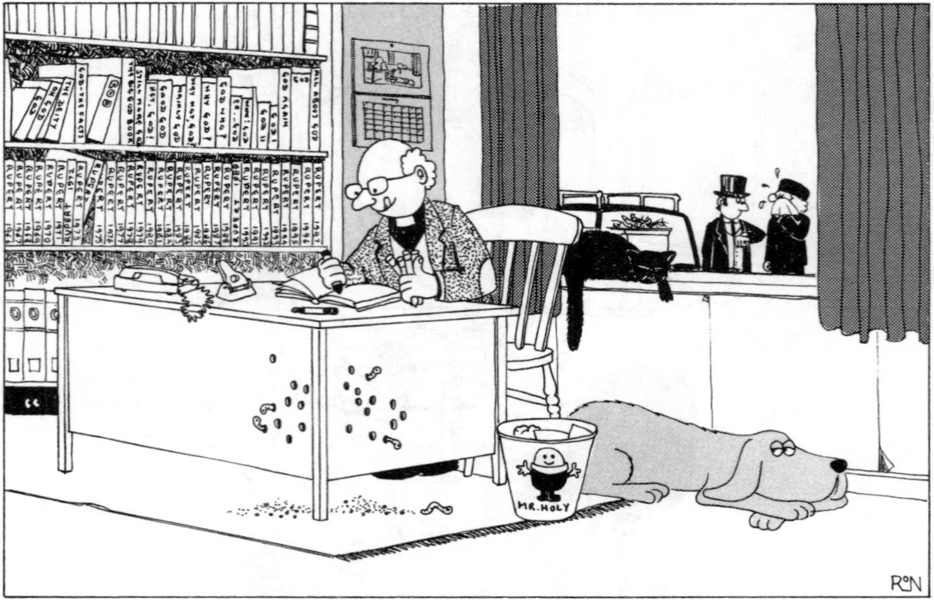
ALL ABOUT GOD
GOD AGAIN
GOD!
GOD II
GOD WHO?
WHY GOD?
WHY NOT, GOD?
MAINLY GOD
GOOD GOD
HEY, GOD!
STILL MORE GOD
THE BIG GOD BOOK
GOD
GOD-THE FACTS
THE DEITY
OH GOD
GOD
RUPERT
MR. HOLY
RON

The Revd Peter Squeals new book made him lose track of time.

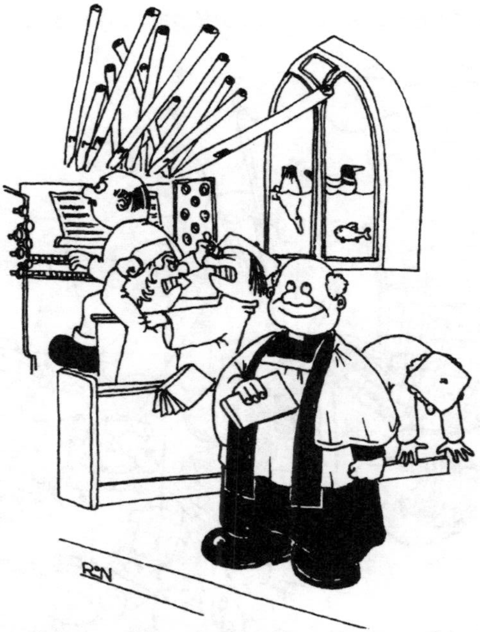
RON

The Reverend Gerry Mentleman let nothing him dismay.

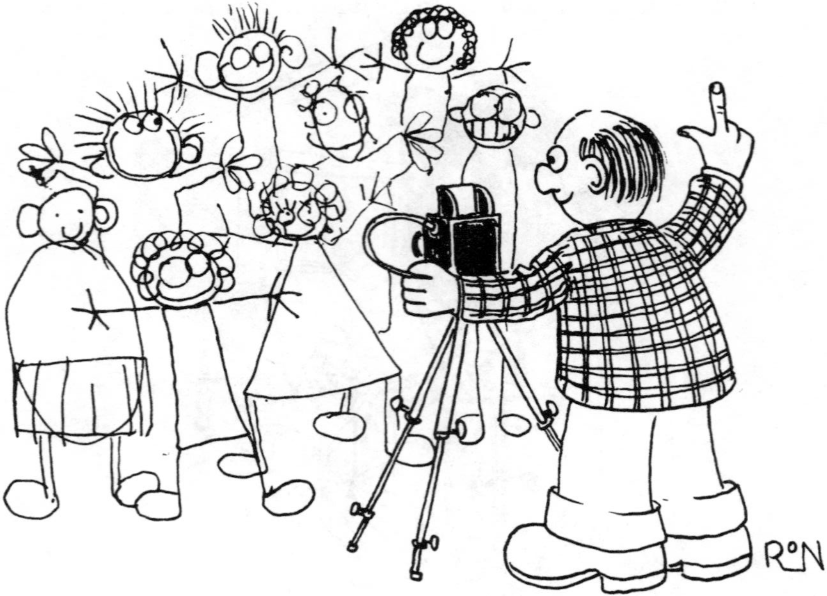
RON

The Sunday School posed for their fundraising tea-towel.

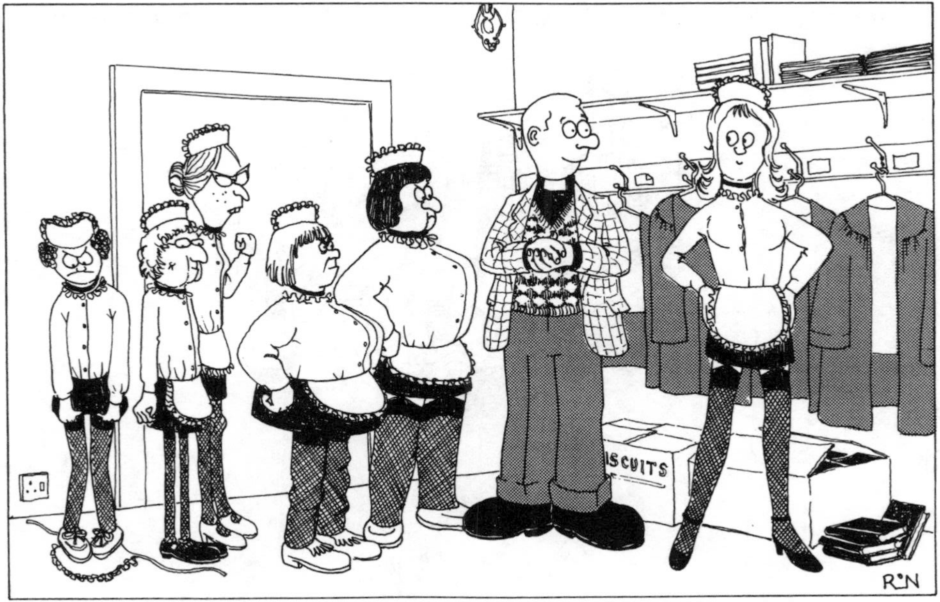
ISCUITS
R.N

The new choir uniform was not an unqualified success.

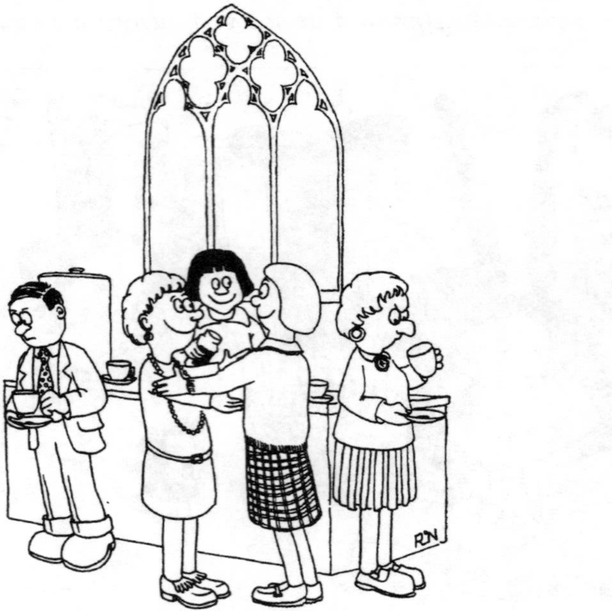
RJN

One hundred and twenty cups from a 200g jar – a personal best and equal to the record!

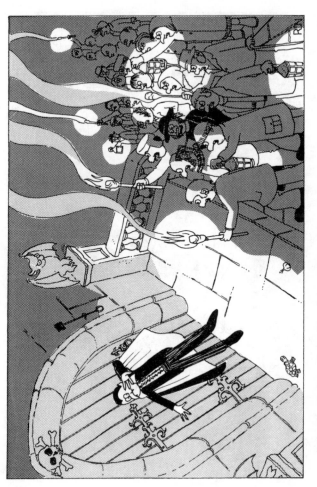

Escape was impossible! The Count had to listen to 'Away in a manger'.

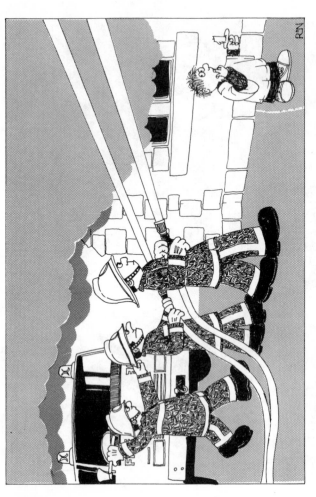

Carols by Candlelight had seemed like a good idea at the time.

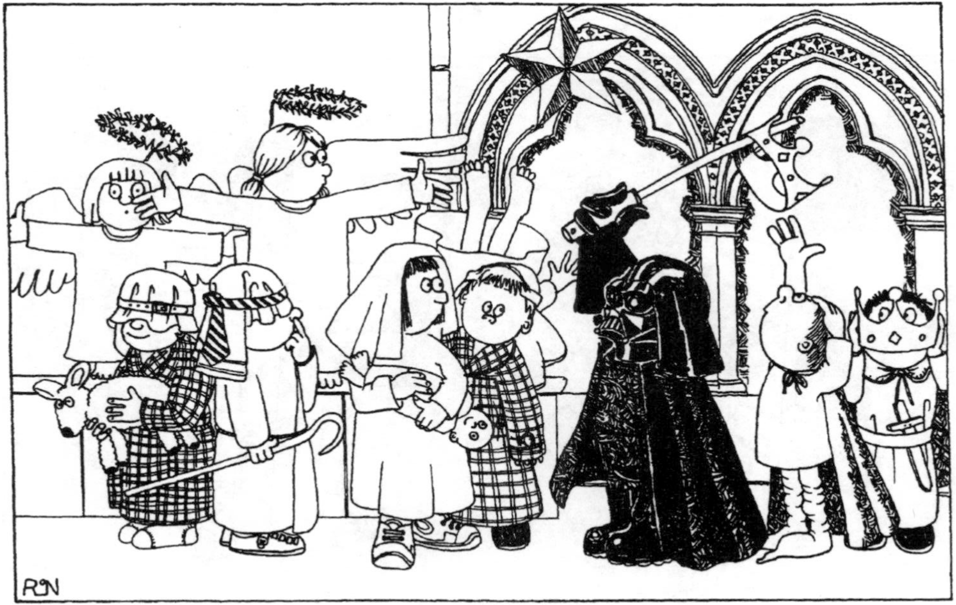
RJN

Ronnie refused to be in the play unless he could be Darth Vader.

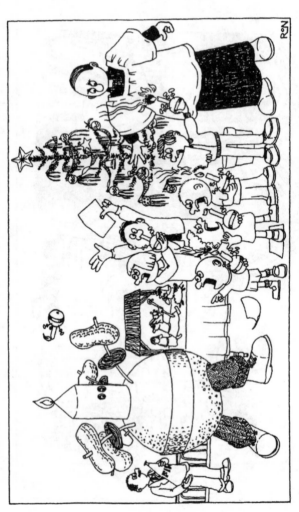

The climax of the service was the arrival of Mr Christingle.

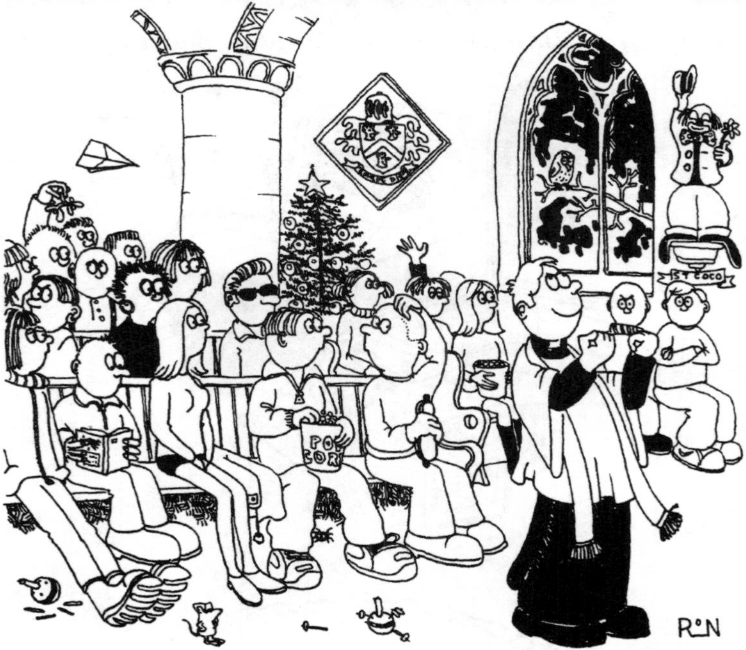
ST COCO
POP
CORN
RON

Someone had spread it around that Midnight Mass was a horror movie.

Straight after Christmas dinner, Peter started work on the Lent course.

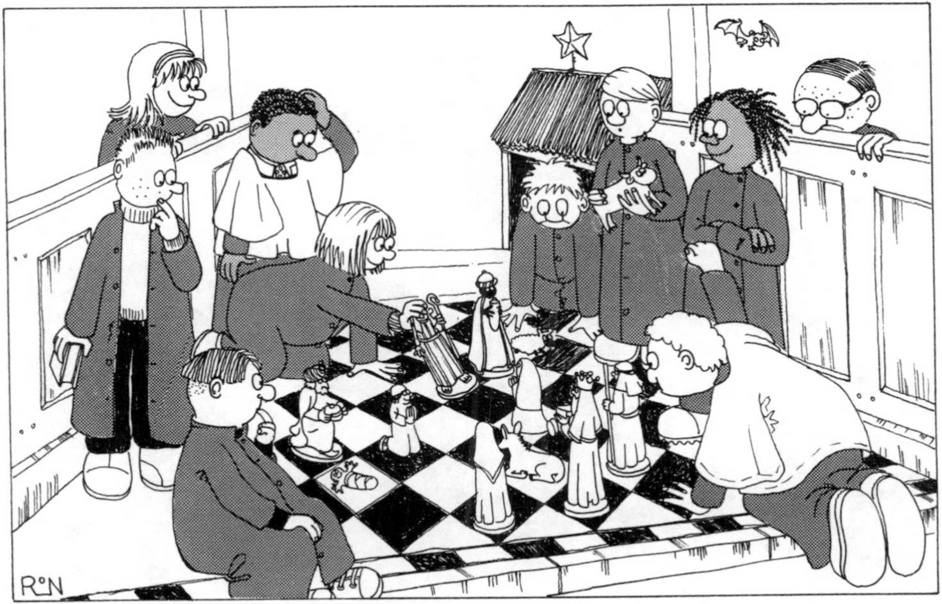
RoN

The choir enjoyed their annual game of crib.

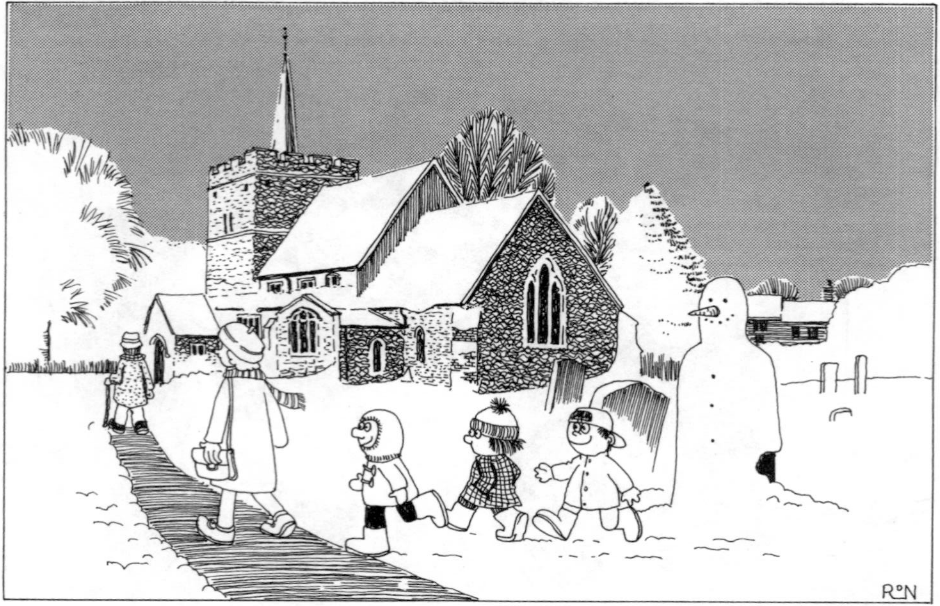
RoN

The Vicar had not been seen since the Sunday School Christmas party.

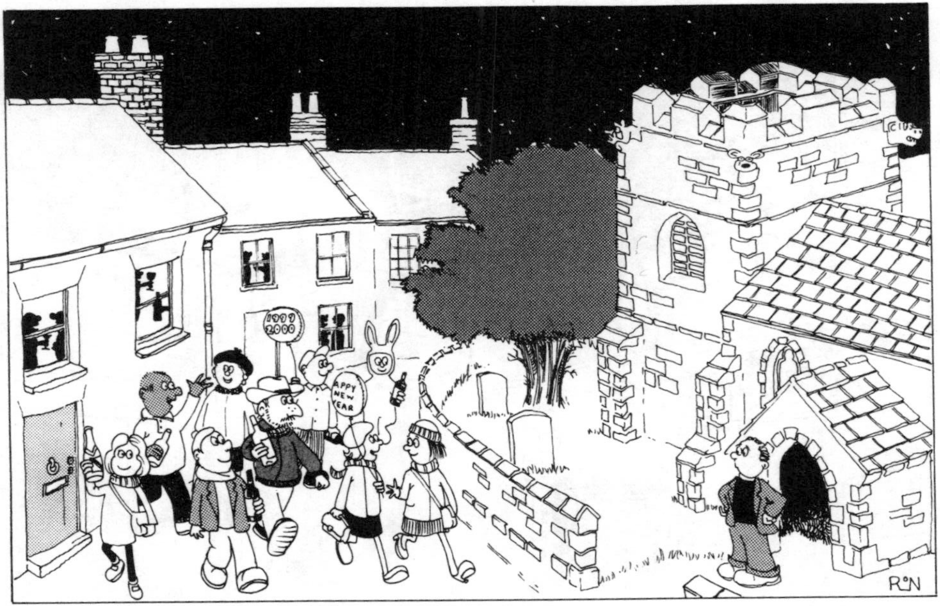
1999
2000
APPY
NEW
YEAR
RON

Mortimer wondered if anyone would come to the Watch Night service.

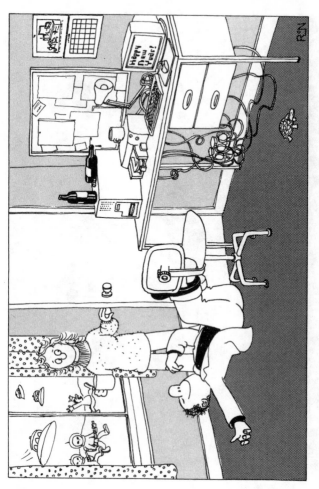

As the millennium bug struck, the computer was fine – but Peter crashed.

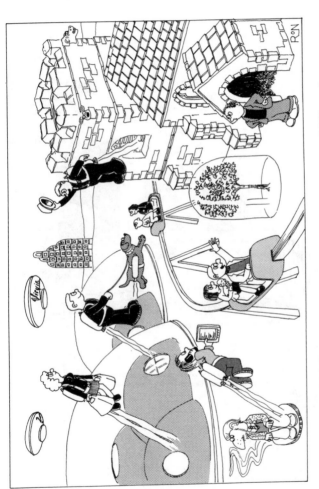

Mortimer emerged from church to greet the new Millennium.

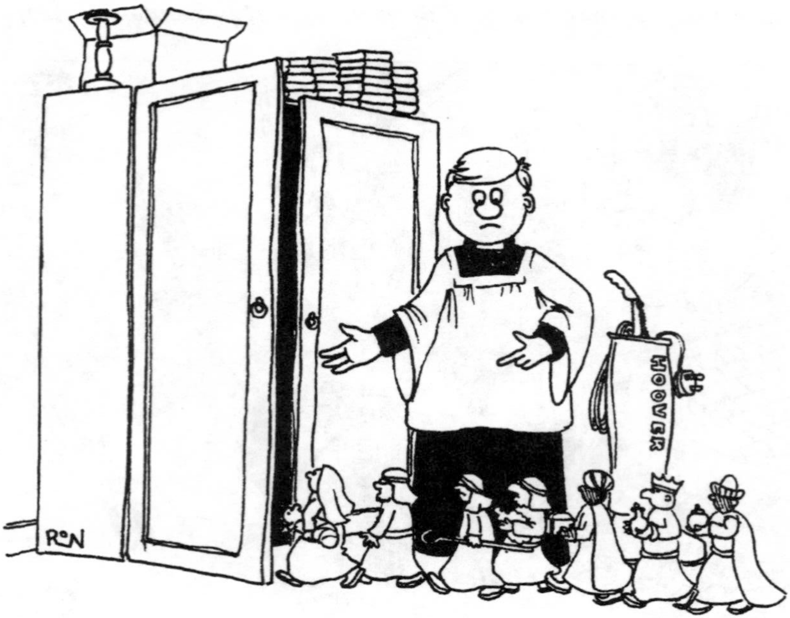
HOOVER
RON

. . . so it was back for another year in the vestry cupboard.

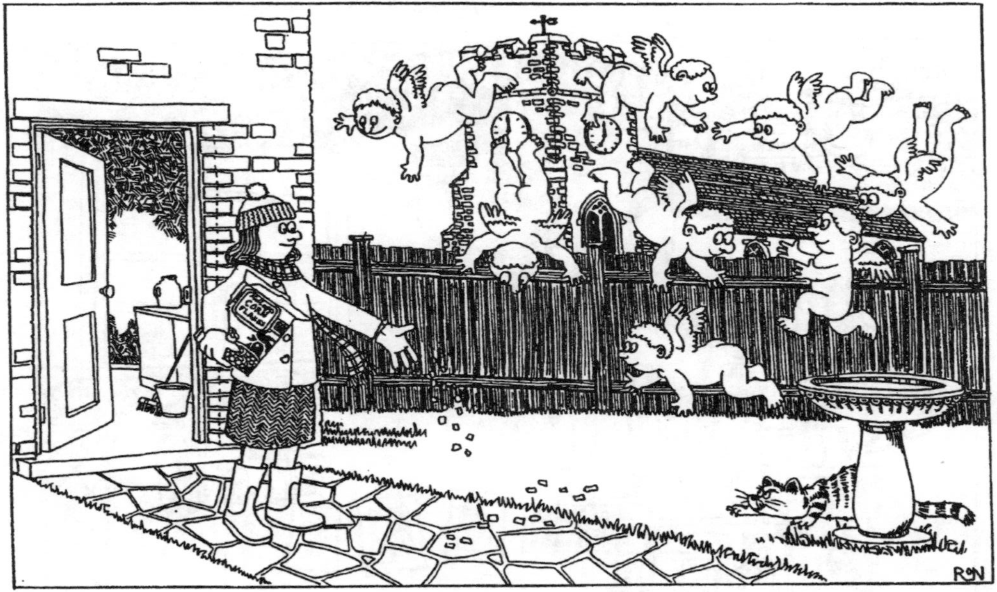
CORN FLAKES
RON

The Vicar's wife helped the cherubim through the worst of the winter.

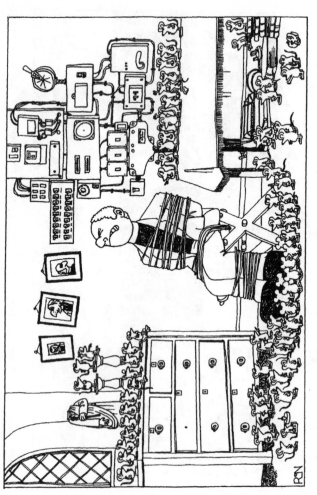

Gregory steadfastly refused to divulge the whereabouts of the cheese.

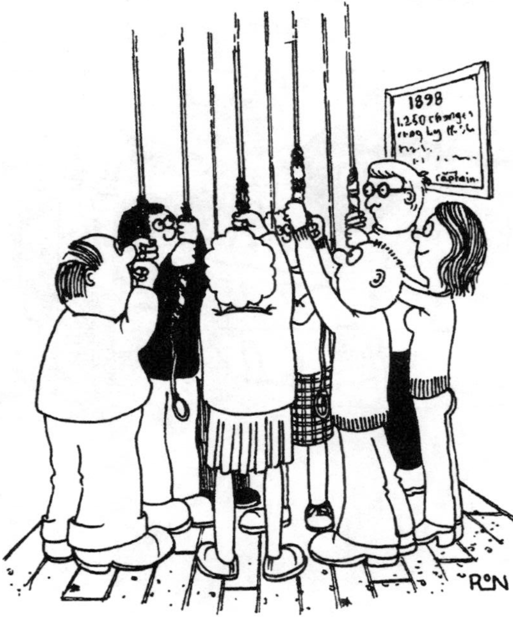
1898
RON

When boredom set in, they played 'Mr Tambourine Man'.

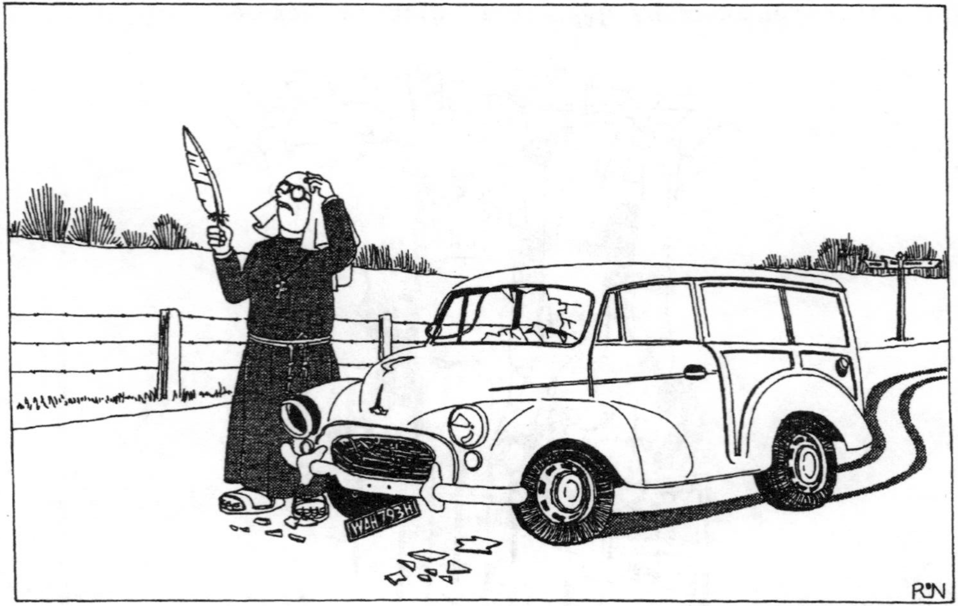
WAH 793H

Sister Sarah's encounter with an angel left her shaken and confused.

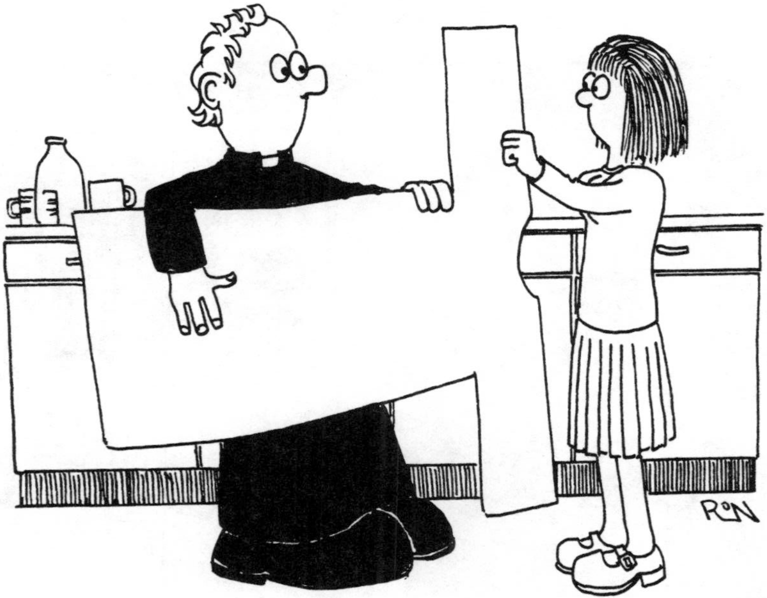
RON

Clarence put in a plea for a little less starch.

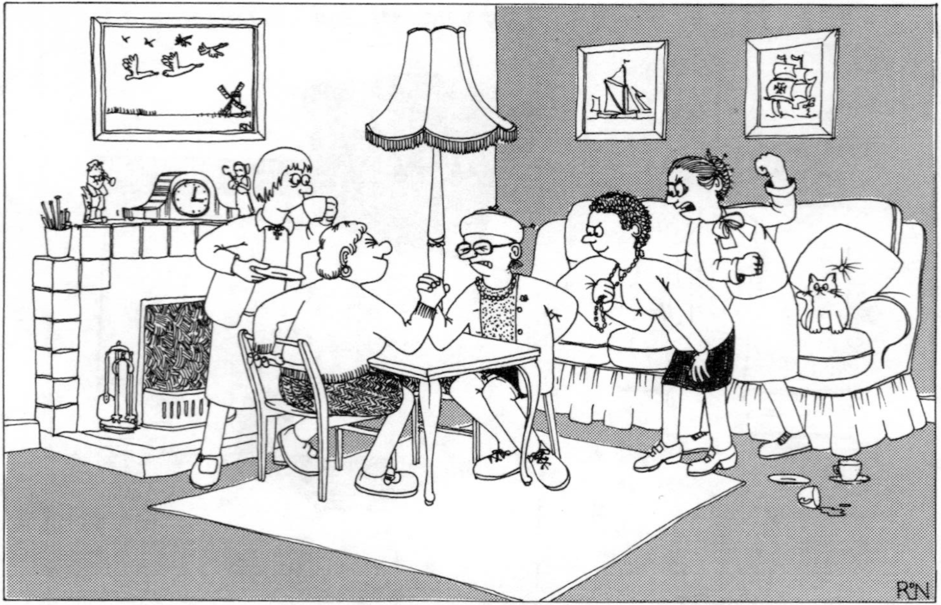

The Mother's Union chose a new Enrolling Member.

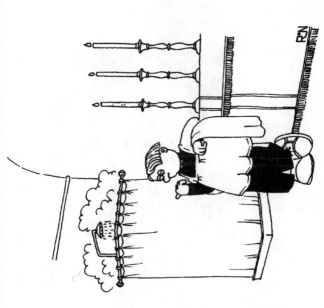

The Revd Saul Pope considered the ablution a vital part of the Liturgy.

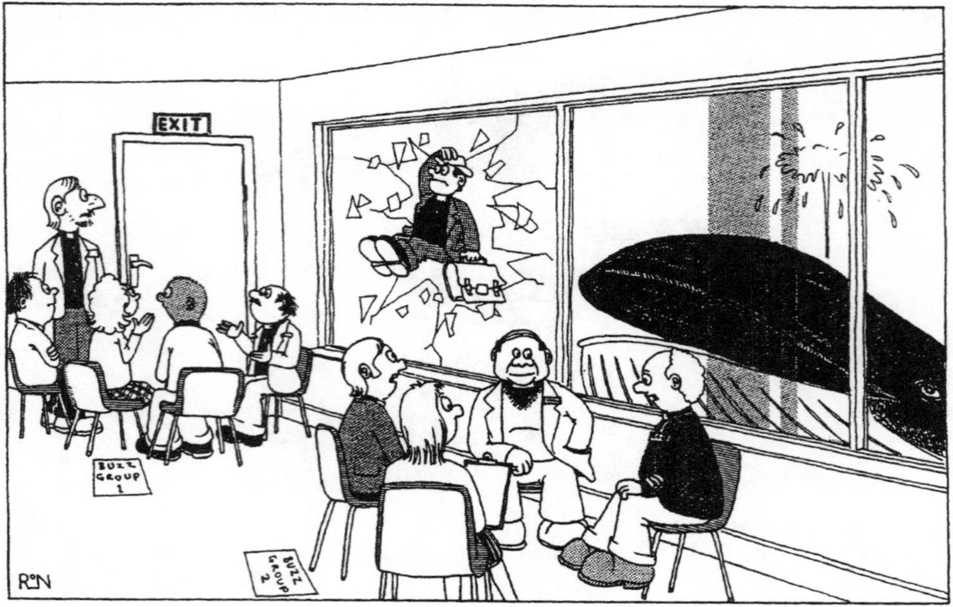
EXIT
BUZZ GROUP 1
BUZZ GROUP 2
RON

The Revd Jonah Crackers reluctantly joined the others at the clergy conference.

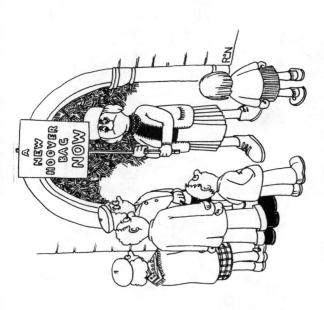

Few dared to cross Mrs Threadgold's picket line.

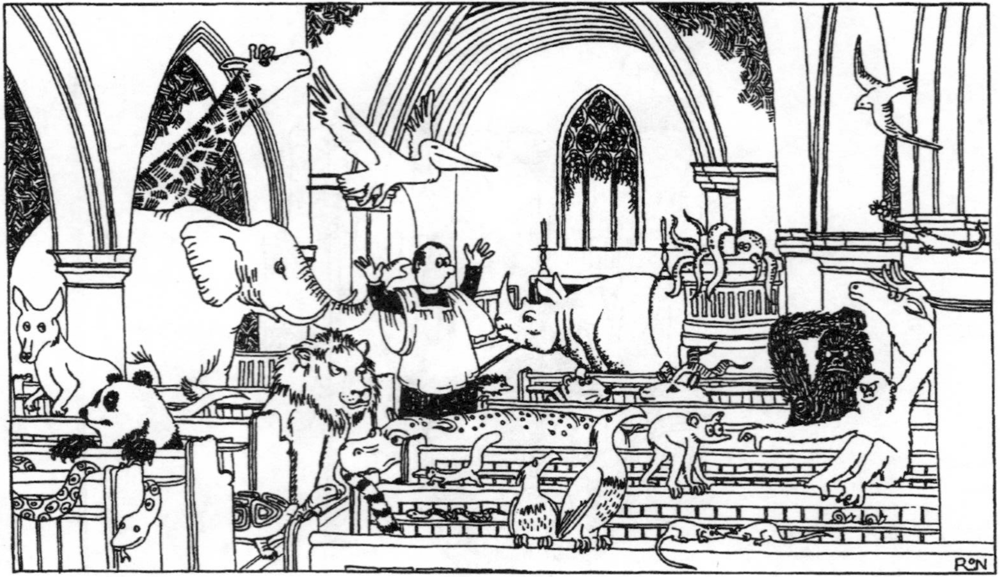
RJN

Bats were not a problem.

Hilary found that Jean was wearing the same outfit.

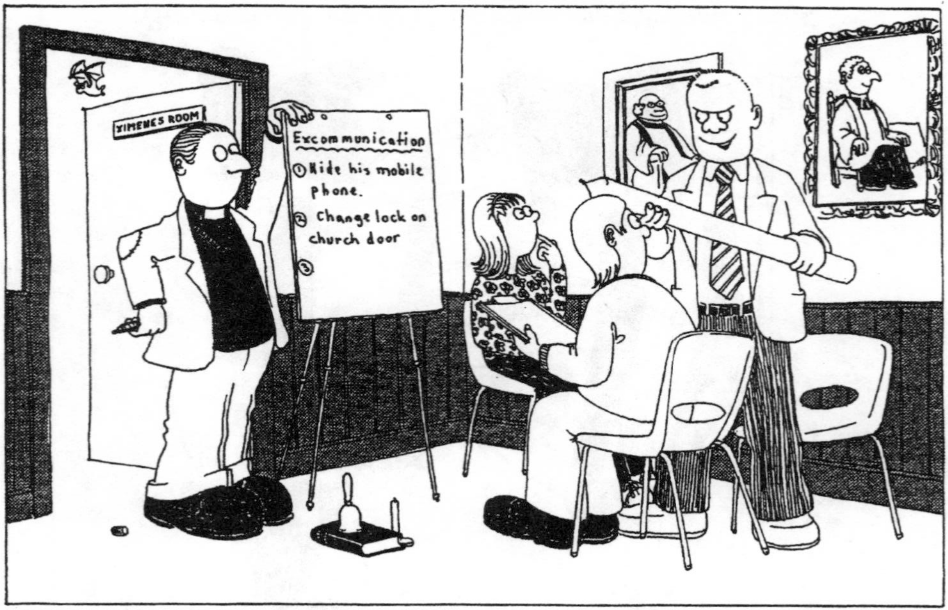
XIMENES ROOM
Excommunication
① Hide his mobile phone.
② Change lock on church door
③

'Just give me a big enough candle,' said James, 'and I won't need a bell or a book!'

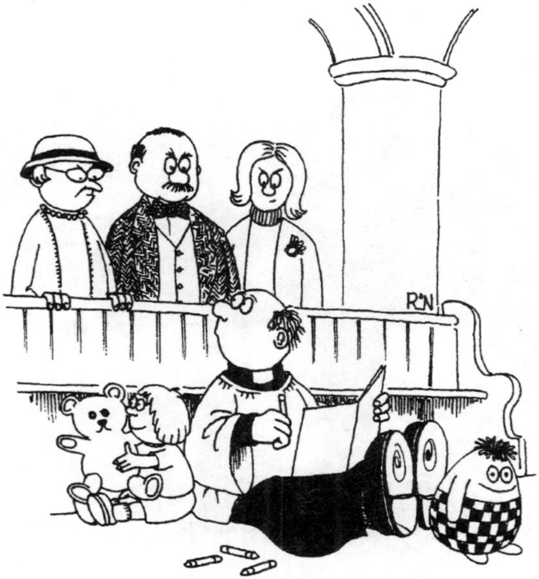
R'N

For little ones who got bored, there were soft toys and crayons.

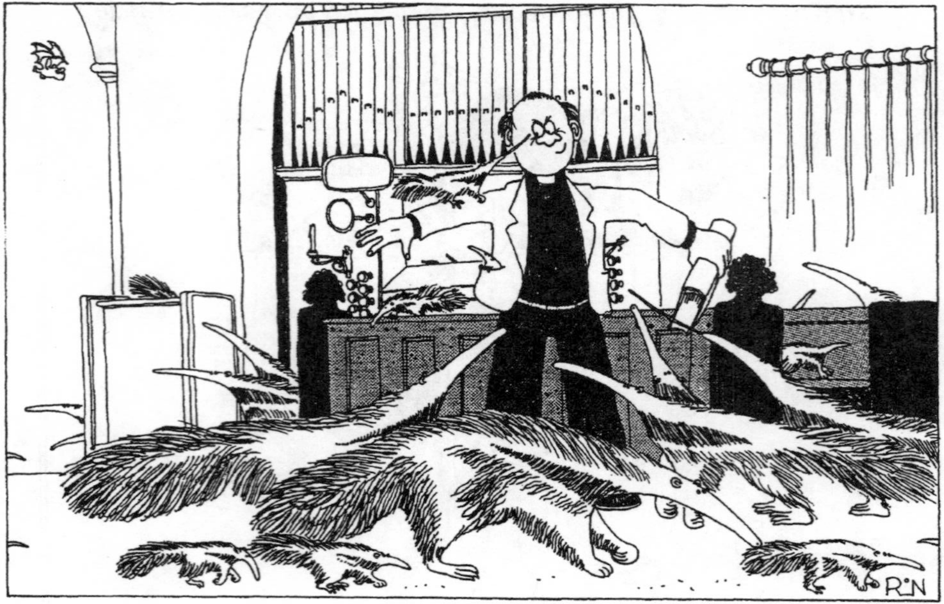
R.N

Sometimes Eric thought he would have been better off with the ants.

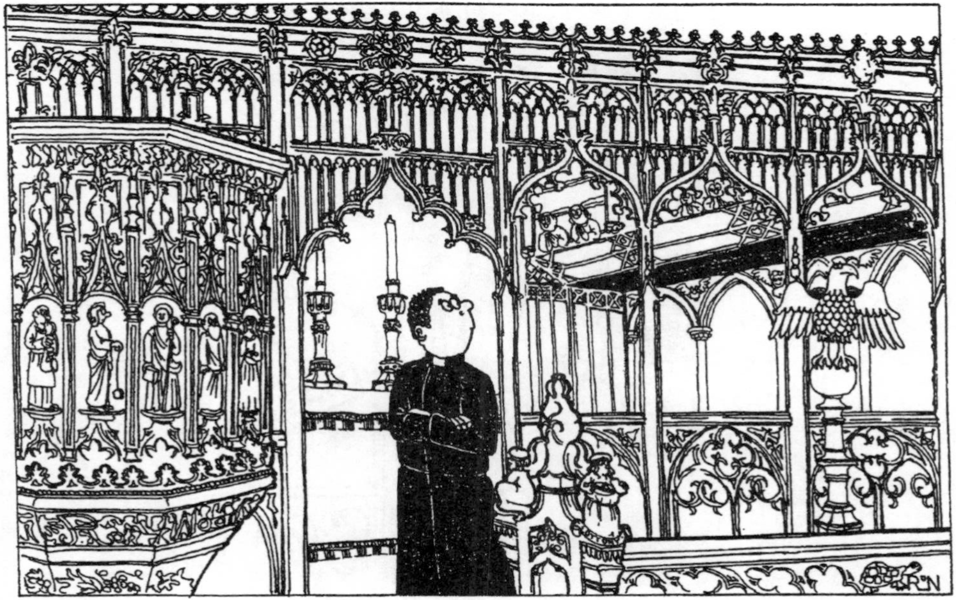

The Revd Midge Fragnetts missed the flowers during Lent.

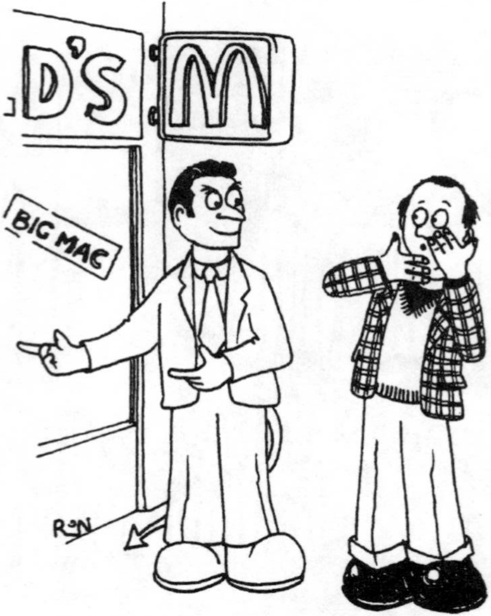
D'S
M
BIG MAC
RON

The Lenten fast began to take hold.

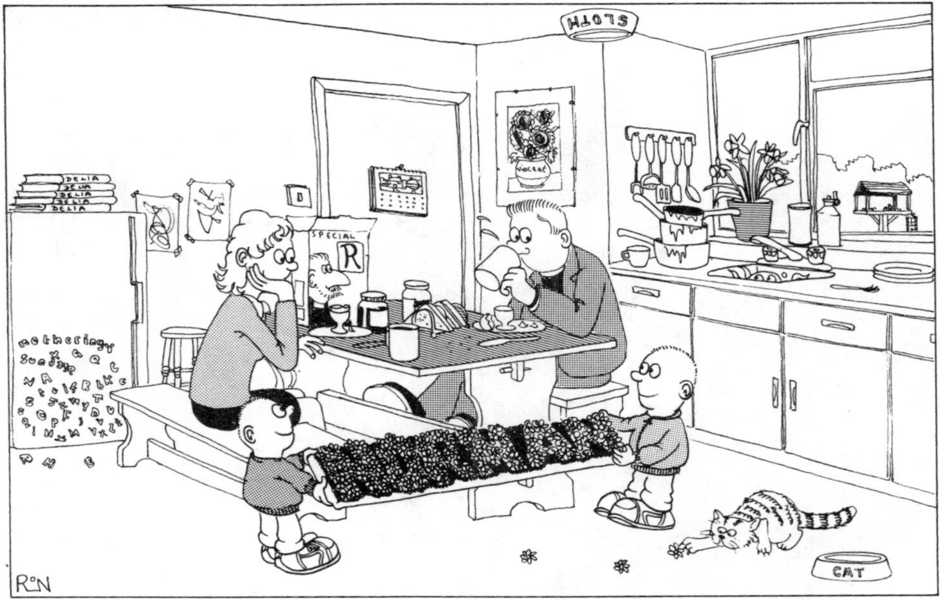
SLOTH
DELIA
SPECIAL
R
CAT
RON

The twins picked Mummy some pretty flowers from the churchyard.

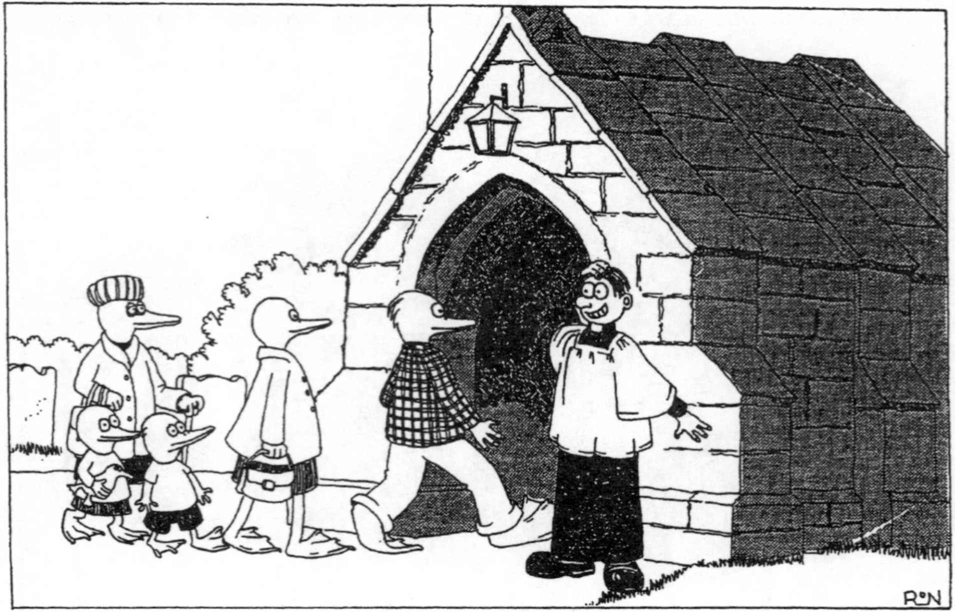
RON

Throughout Lent, Michael had fantasies about his favourite Chinese food.

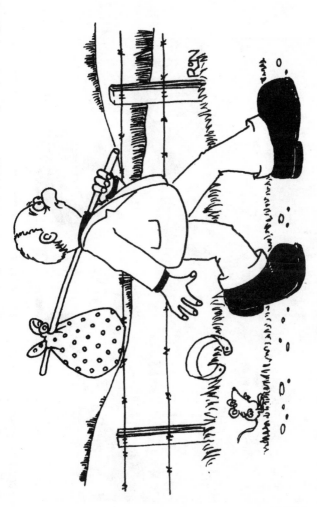

And then, one Lent, Basil simply gave up.

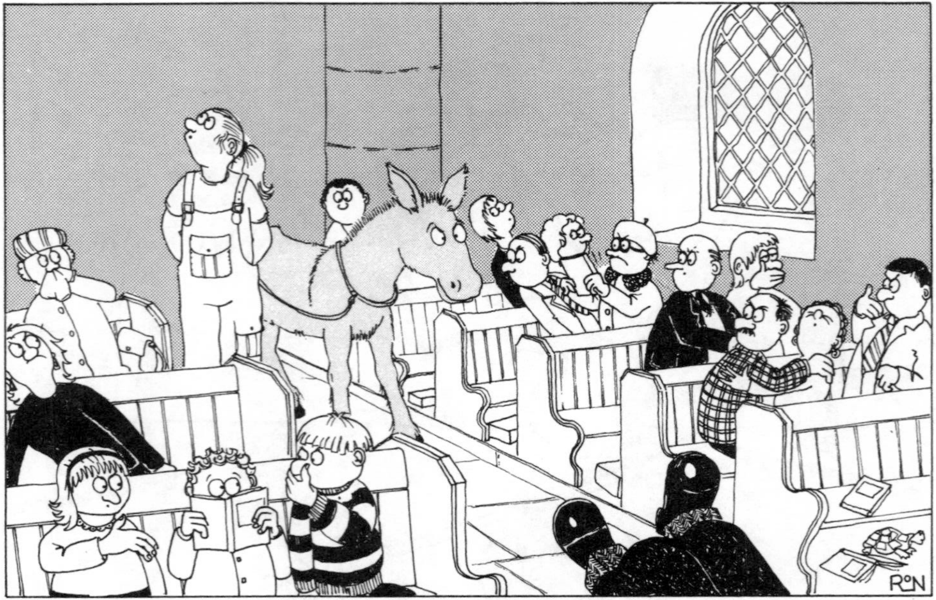
RON

A real live donkey added considerably to the atmosphere on Palm Sunday.

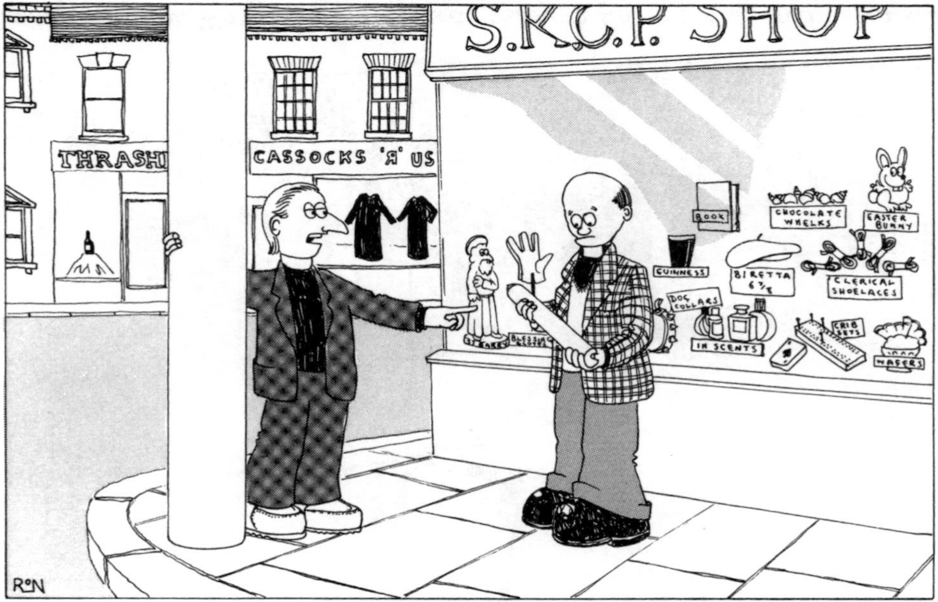
S.K.C.P. SHOP
THRASH
CASSOCKS 'Я' US
BOOK
CHOCOLATE WHELKS
EASTER BUNNY
GUINNESS
BIRETTA 6⅞
CLERICAL SHOELACES
DOG COLLARS
IN SCENTS
CRIB SETS
WAFERS
RON

'Call that a Paschal Candle?' sneered Father Seamus.

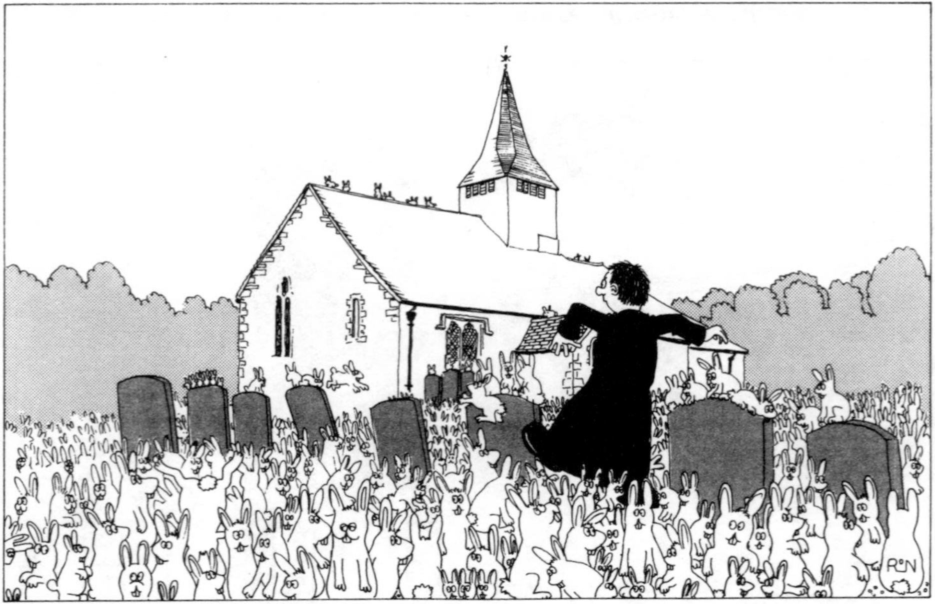
RON

On Easter Sunday, Wayne picked his way through the mass of pagan symbolism.

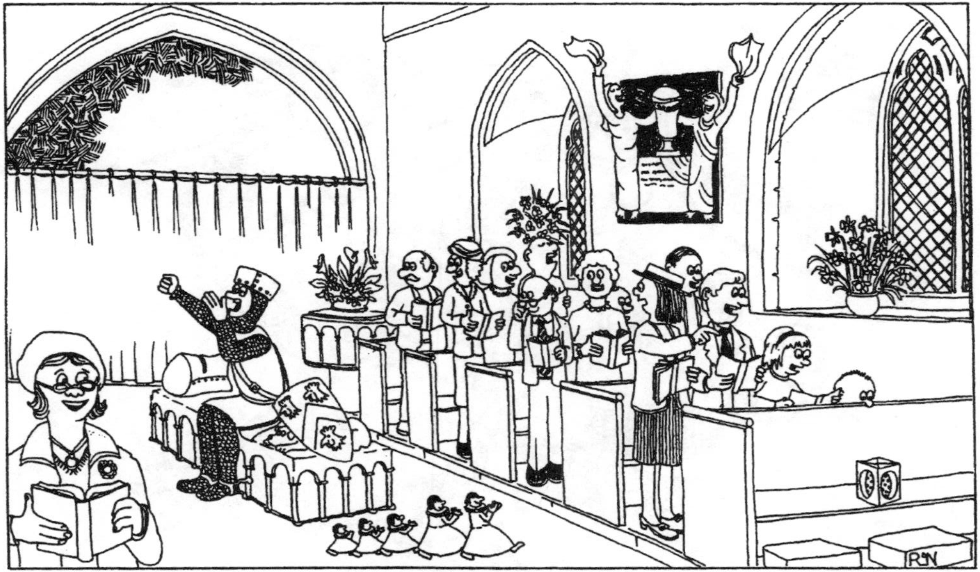

On Easter Sunday morning, the atmosphere in church was quite infectious.

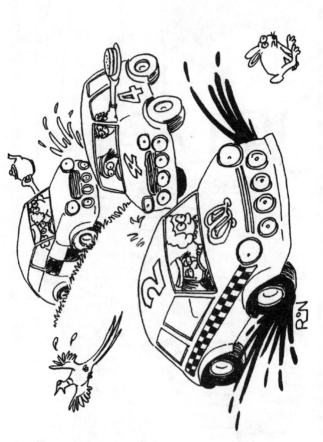

The Mothers' Union were expected to rally round with tea and cake.

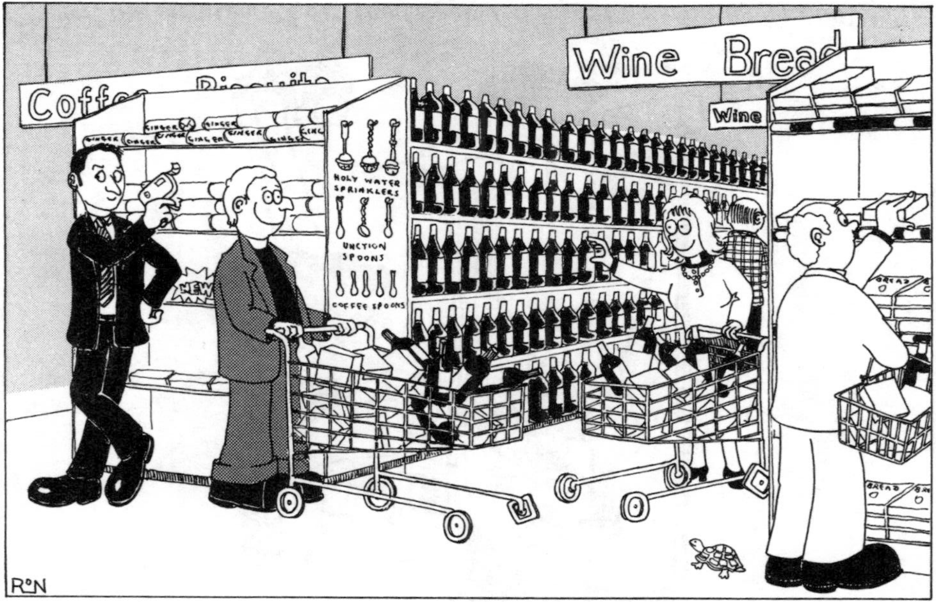
Wine
Bread
Wine
HOLY WATER SPRINKLERS
UNCTION SPOONS
COFFEE SPOONS
NEW
RON

Romance blossomed in the Wippell's food hall.

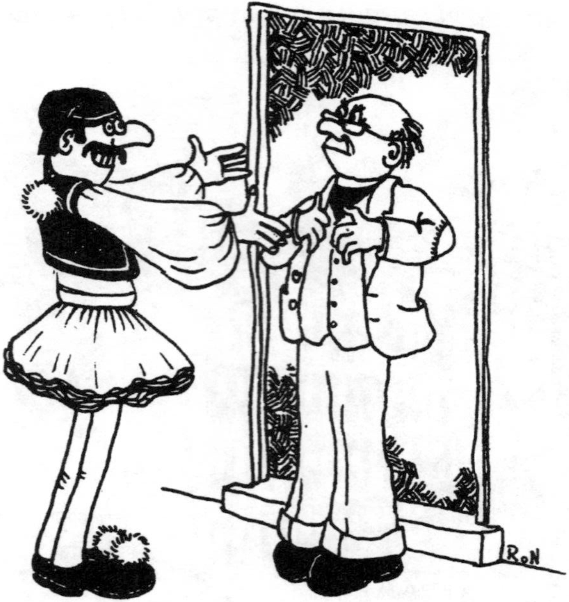
RoN

'Yes', cried the stranger, 'I am the Greek you forgot as soon as you left college.'

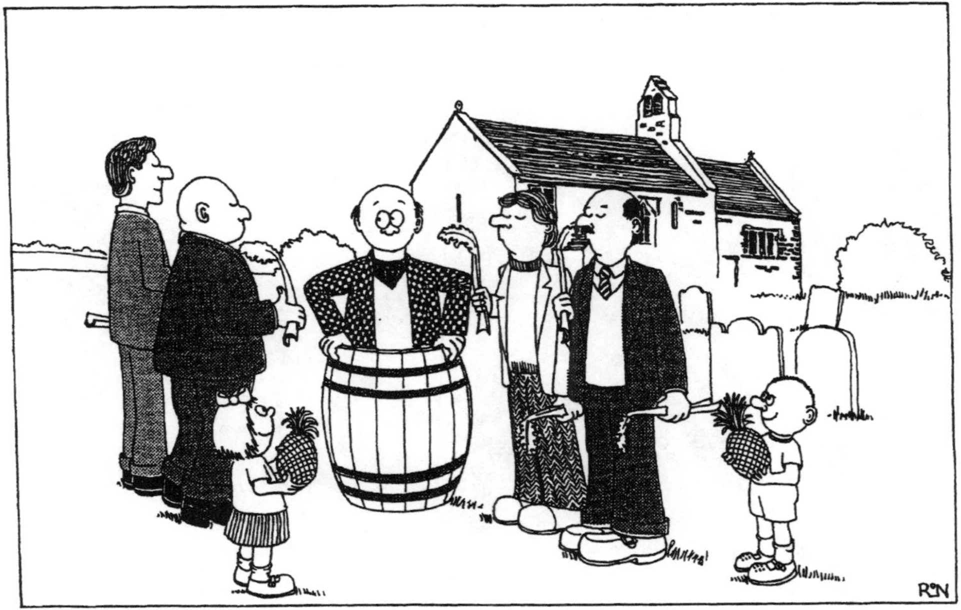
RJN

The Vicar had come to dread the ancient rituals of St Doreen's Day.

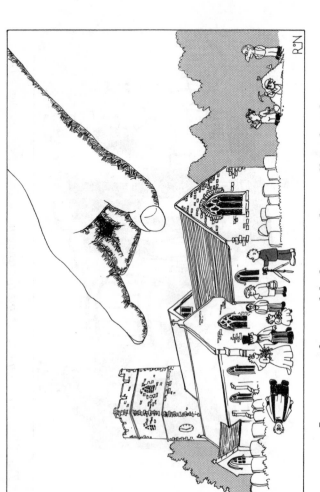

It was a perfect model, down to the smallest detail.

PCC meetings were kept short and to the point.

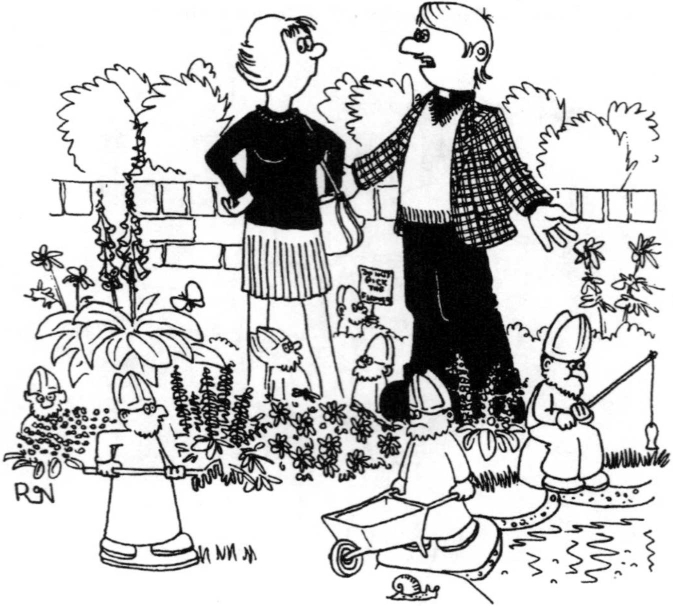
RJN

David showed Doris the celebrated Bishops' garden.

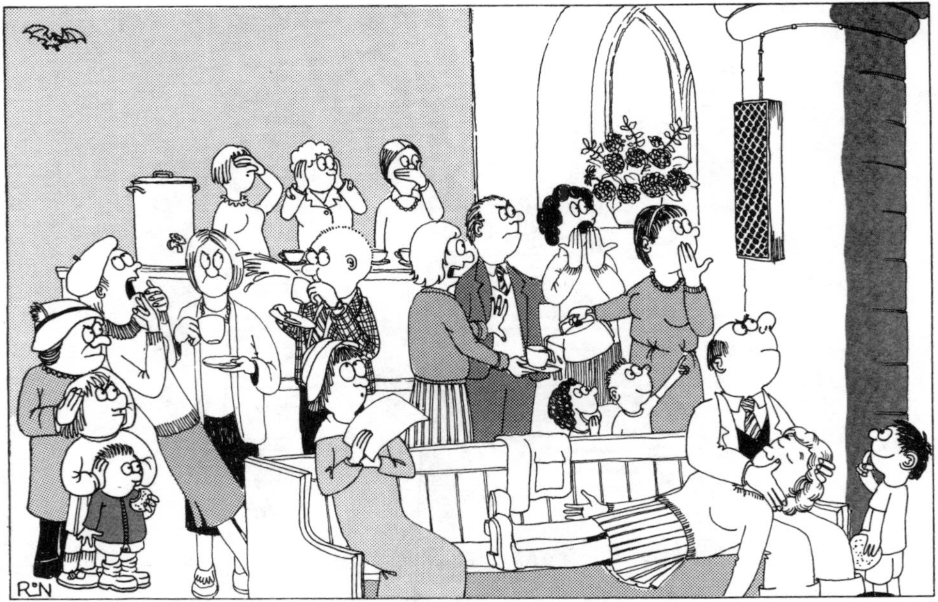
RON

The Vicar returned to the vestry with the radio microphone switched on.

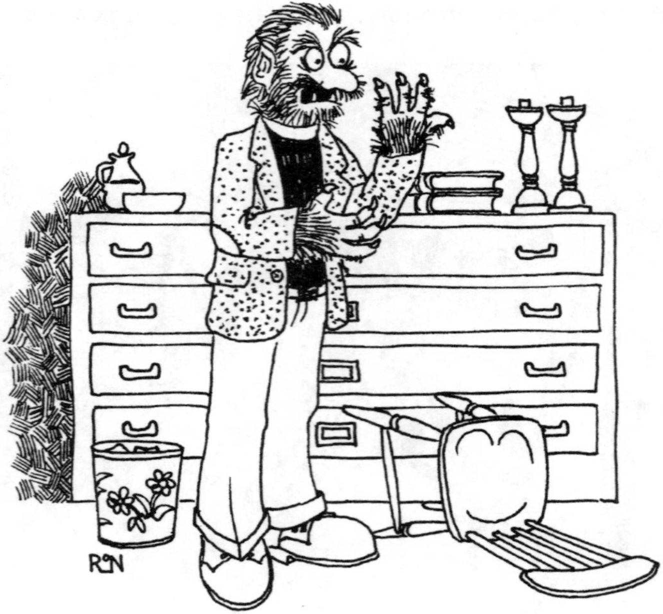

Not just the Altar Frontals changed on Trinity Sunday.

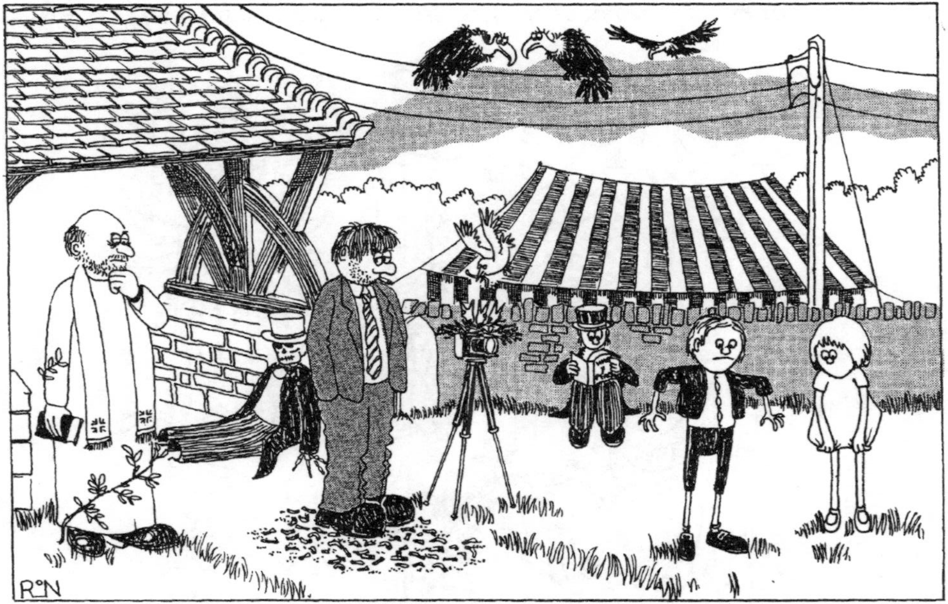
R°N

The bride exercised her privilege to be late.

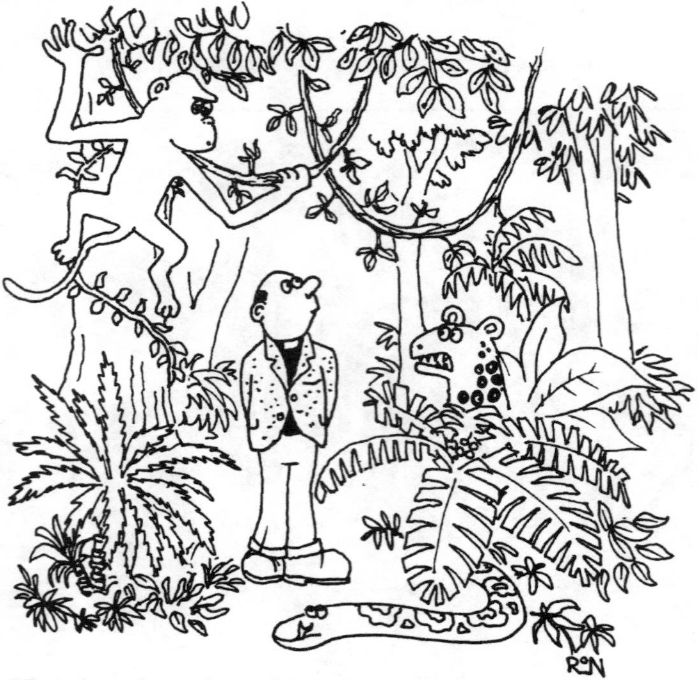
RON

The churchyard working party was never seen again.

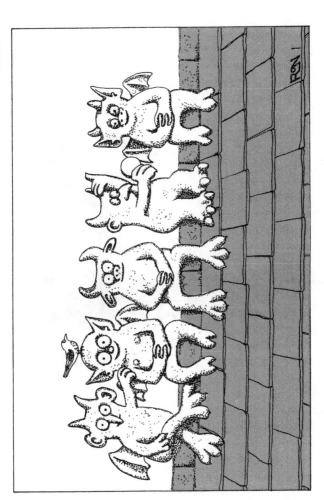

All the gargoyles wanted to look their best for the picture.

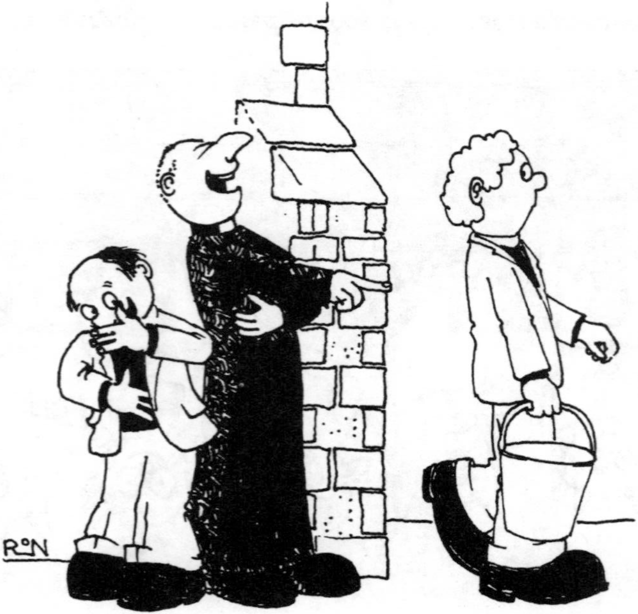
RoN

The new curate was sent for a dozen hail Marys.

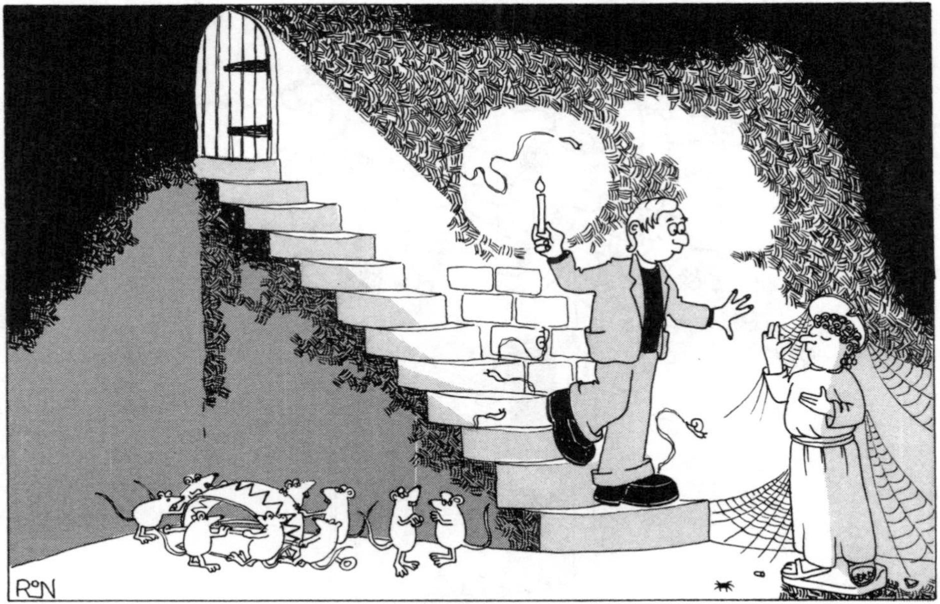

Simon made his annual pilgrimage to the shrine of St Tugnutt the Popular.

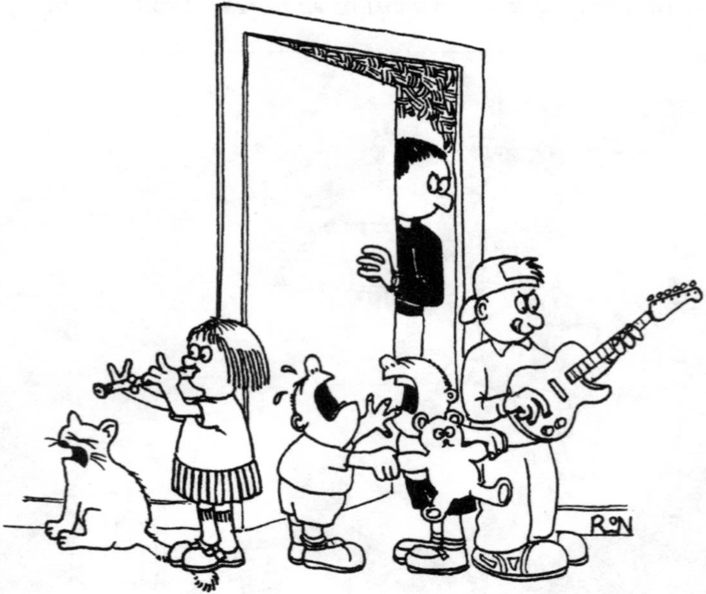
RoN

Kevin took himself off to his study to pray for peace.

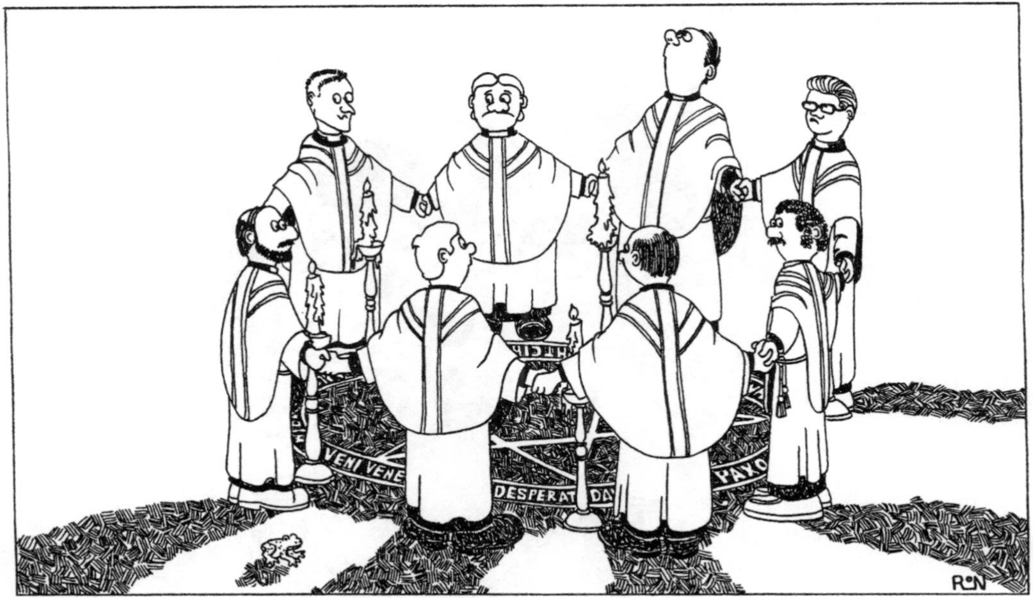
VENI VENE
DESPERAT
PAXO

They waited but the Archdeacon didn't come.

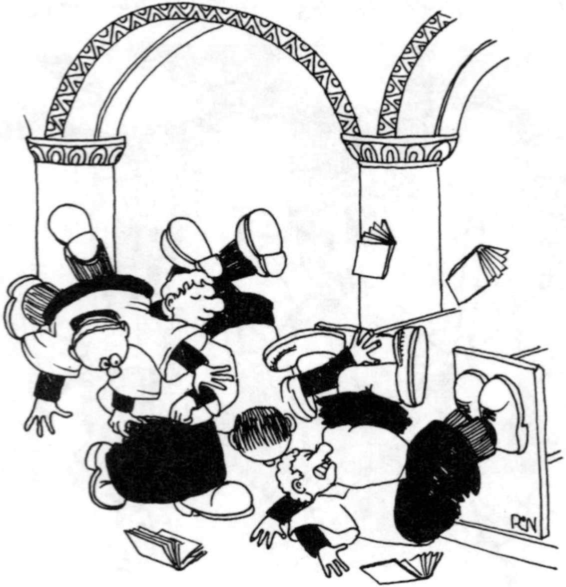
RCN

Barry's genuflexion caught everyone by surprise.

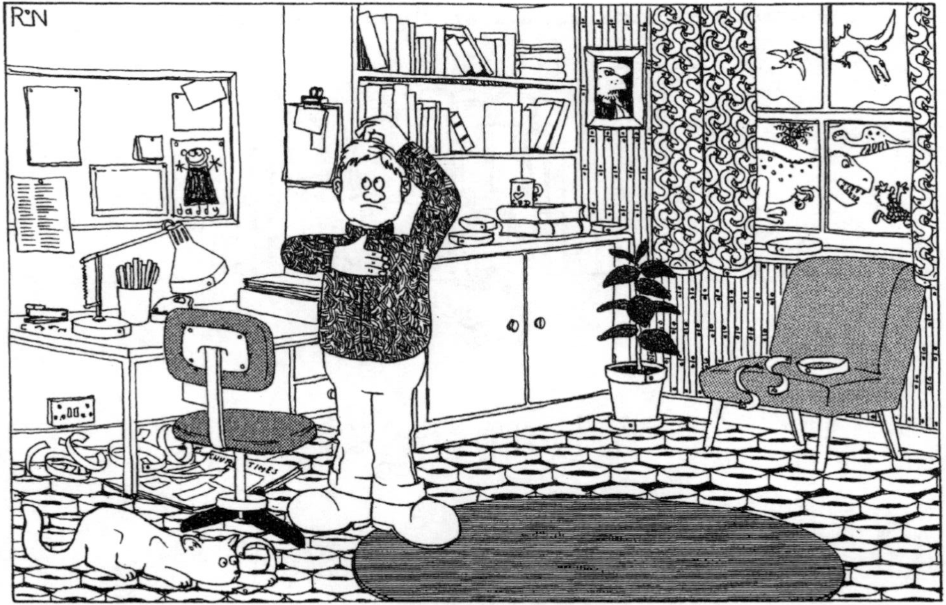
daddy
TIMES

Trevor had dozens of dog collars, but could never find one when he wanted one.

The Bishop spent most of his time in the parishes, encouraging his clergy and their people.

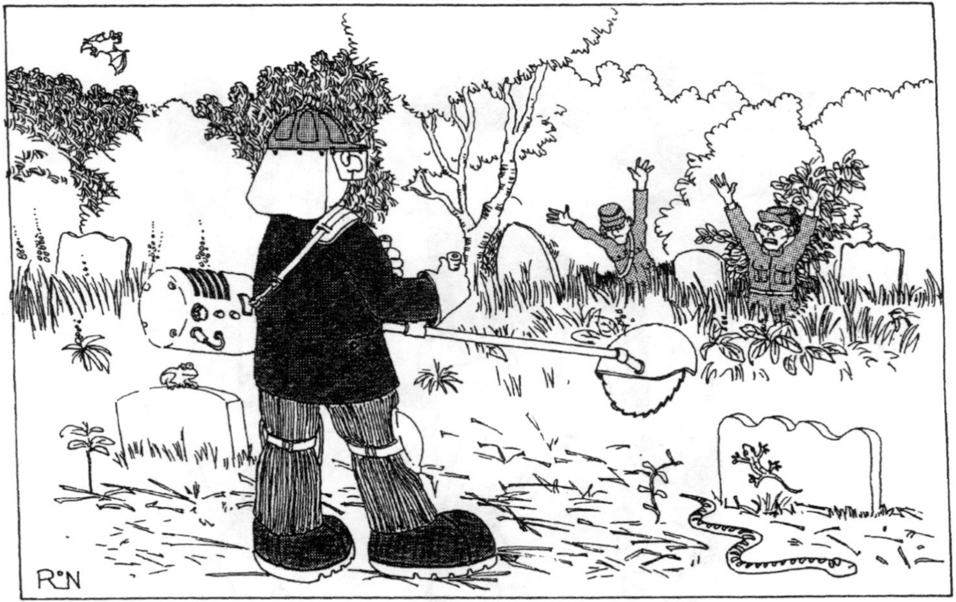
RON

As Melvyn cleared the churchyard, the last Japanese surrendered.

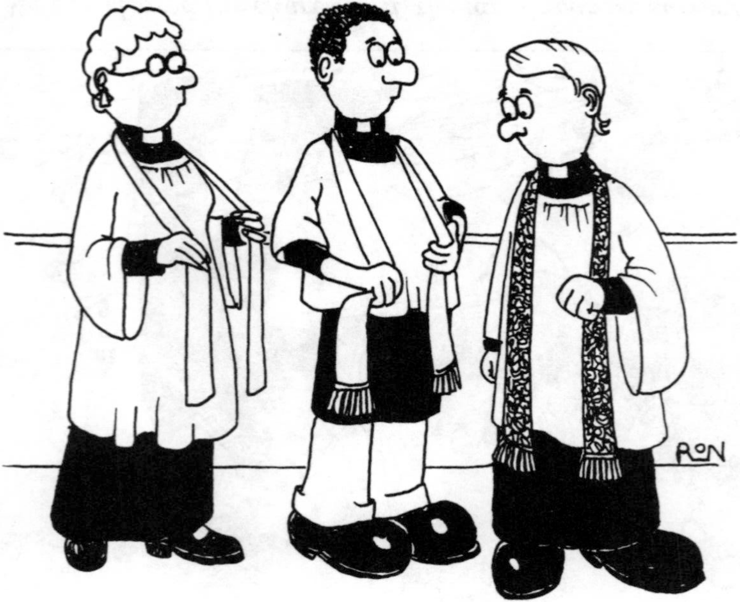
RON

Dennis had been ordained fairly young.

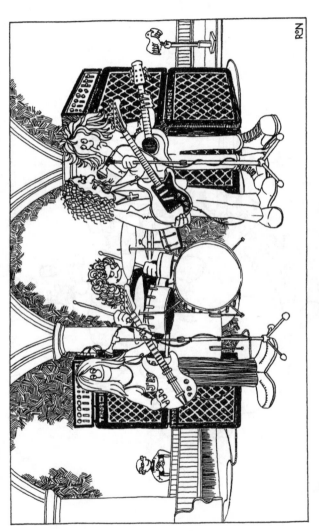

Baz announced Ancient and Modern *number 358 – 'Peace, perfect peace'.*

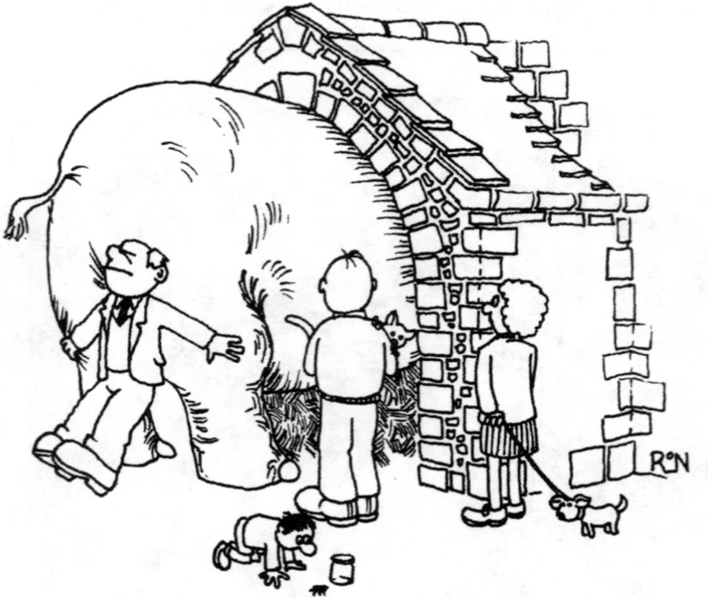
RON

Eventually they decided to hold the pets' service outdoors.

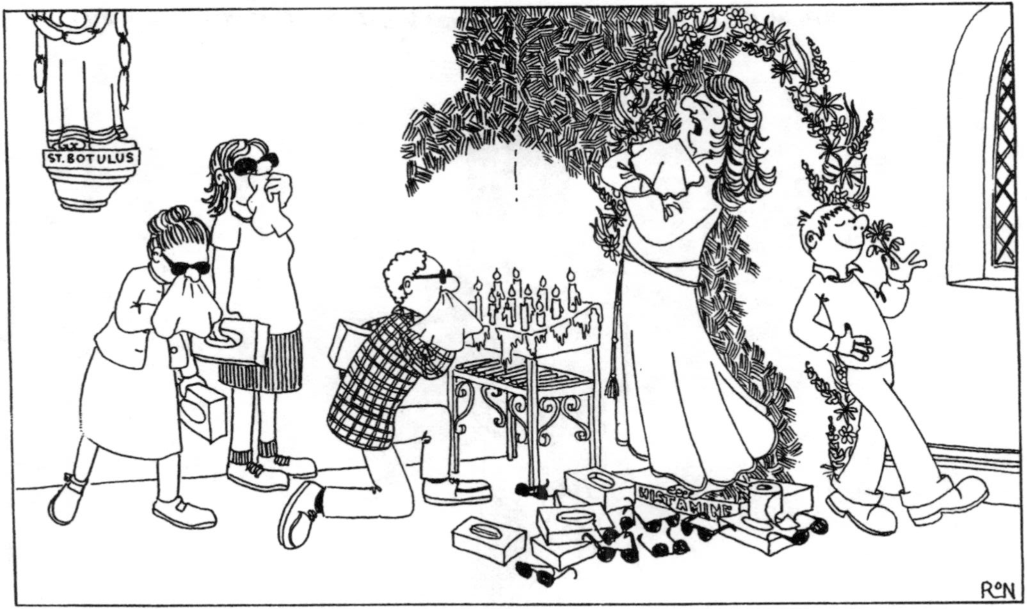
ST. BOTULUS
HISTAMINE
RoN

Hay fever sufferers left their offerings at the shrine of St Histamine.

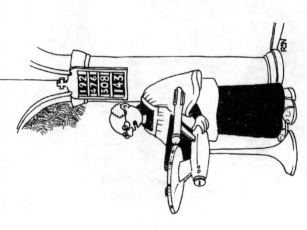

The Vicar spoke at length on 'the eagle – an outmoded medieval symbol.'

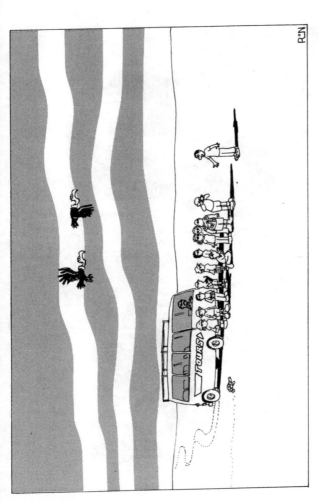

The pilgrims were awestruck when they were shown the actual spot.

71

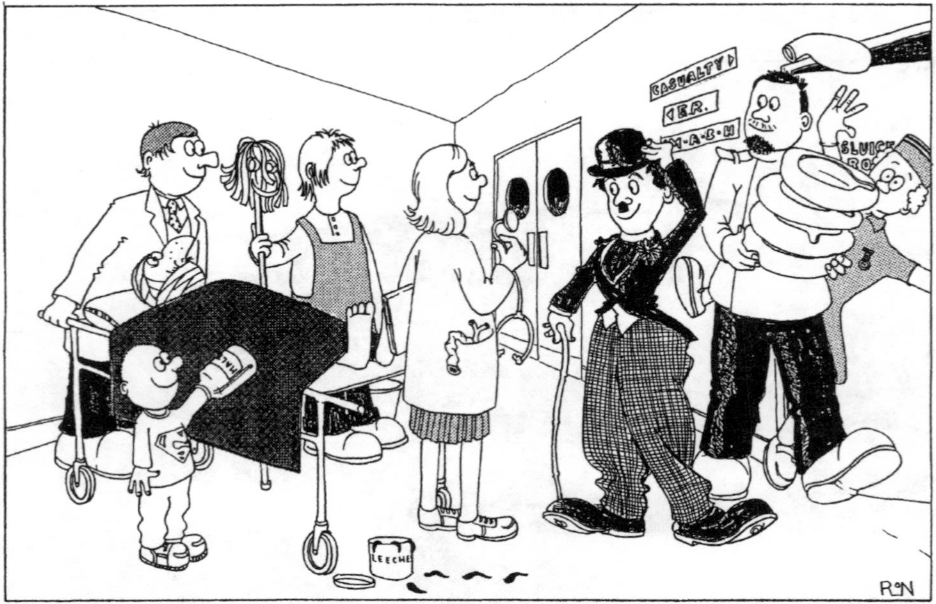
CASUALTY
E.R.
M·A·S·H
RON

Everybody in the hospital was pleased to see the Chaplin.

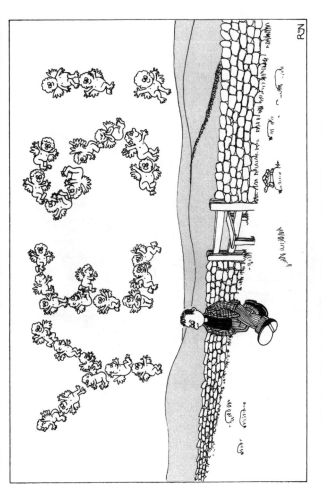

Racked by indecision, Toby sought Divine guidance.

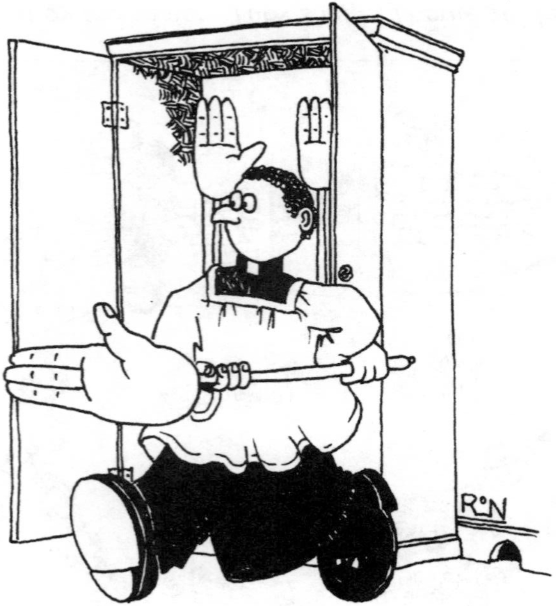
RON

Michael realised this was a case for some heavy duty blessing.

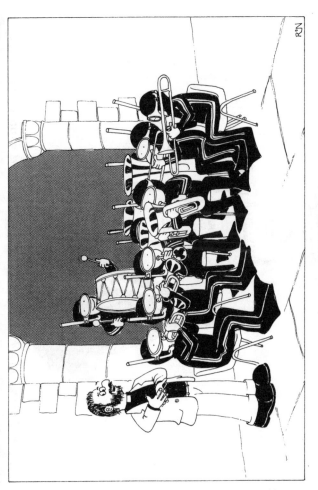

Derek called for a warm welcome for the Band of the Salvation Navy.

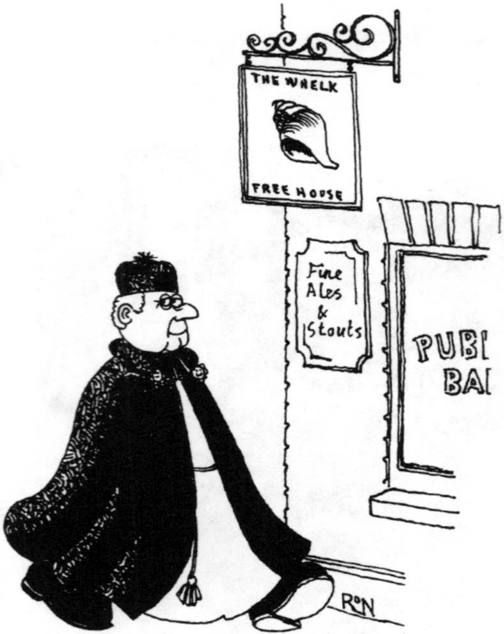
THE WHELK
FREE HOUSE
Fine Ales & Stouts
PUB
BA
RON

At the end of the day, he took off his dog-collar, and slipped out incognito.

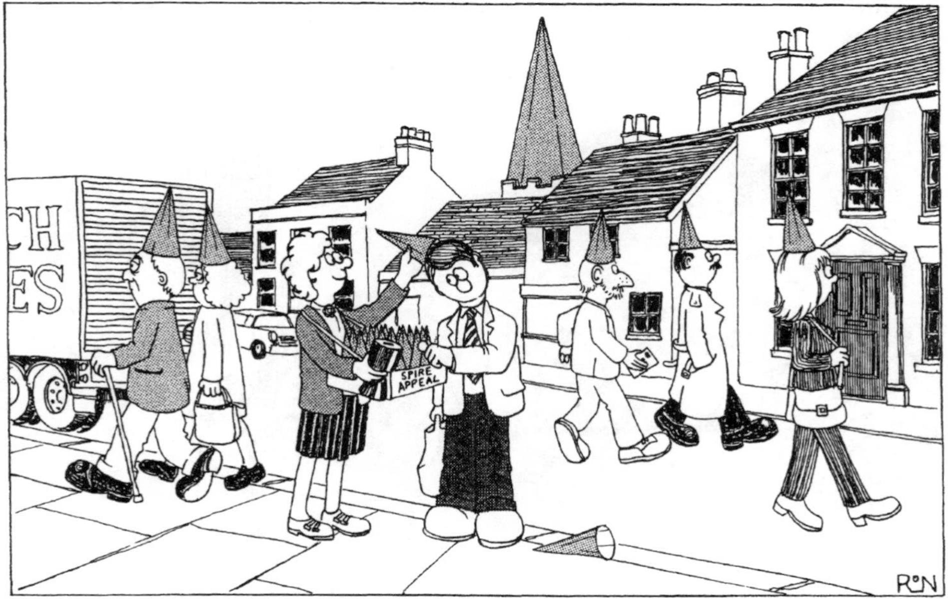
CH
ES
SPIRE APPEAL
RON

It started when someone said flag days were old hat.

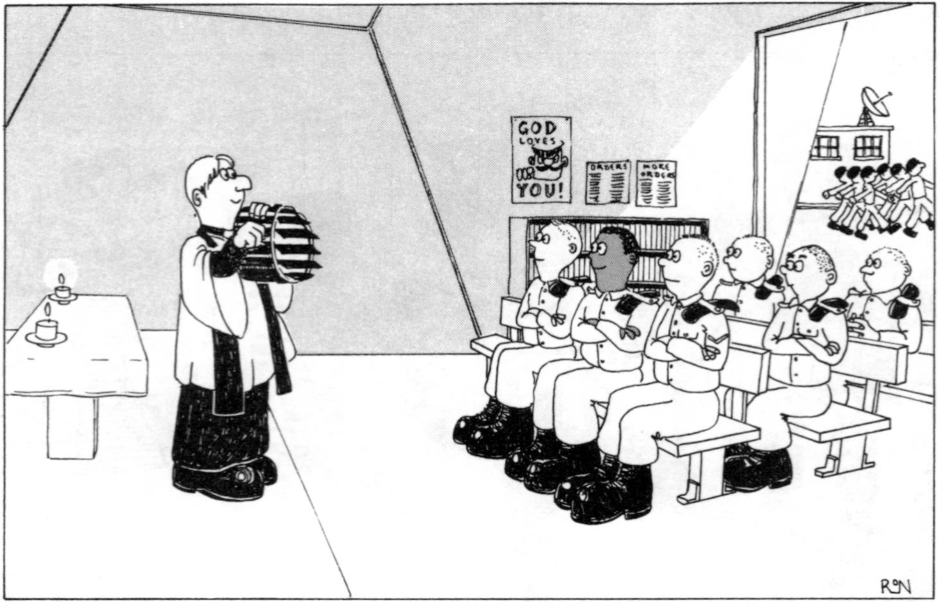
GOD LOVES YOU!
ORDERS
MORE ORDERS
RON

Laryngitis did not deter the Chaplain to the Royal Corps of Signals.

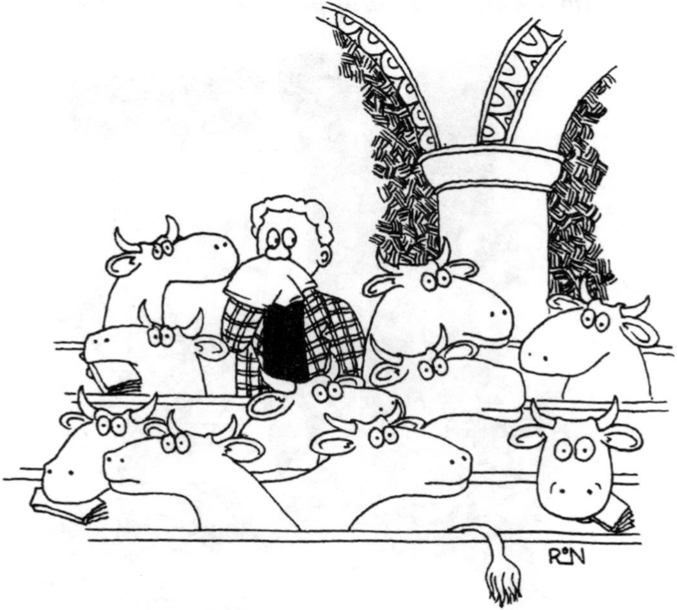
RON

The Reverend Crispin Batter had no idea about the laws of sanctuary.

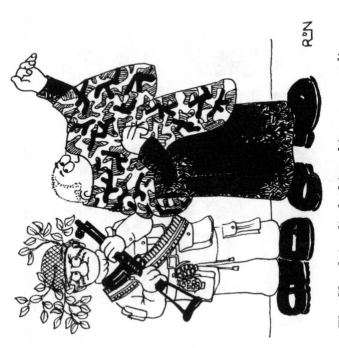

The Chaplain climbed into his army surplice.

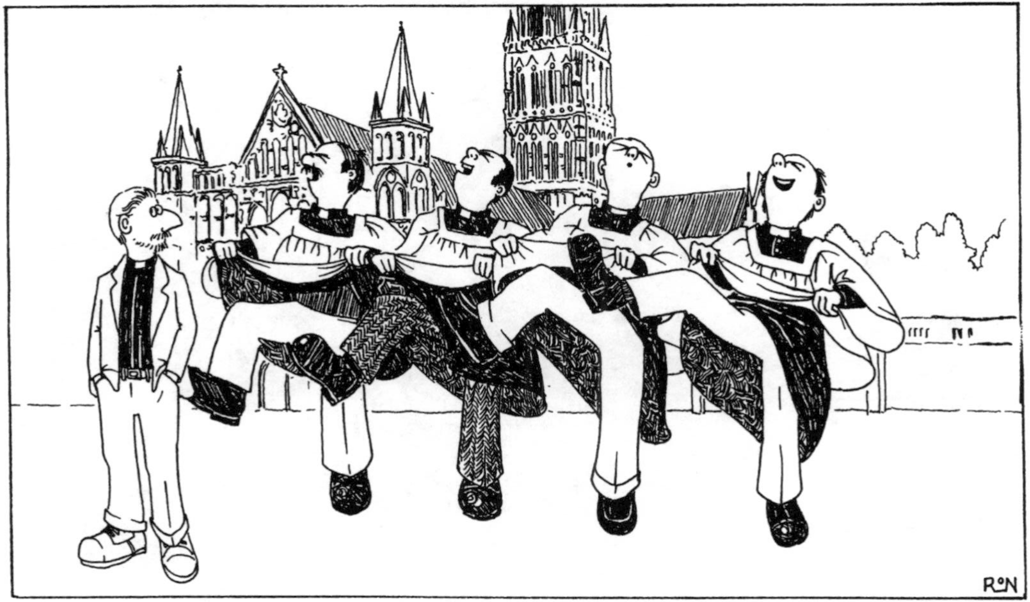
RON

The Church Times *cartoonist was seldom short of inspiration.*

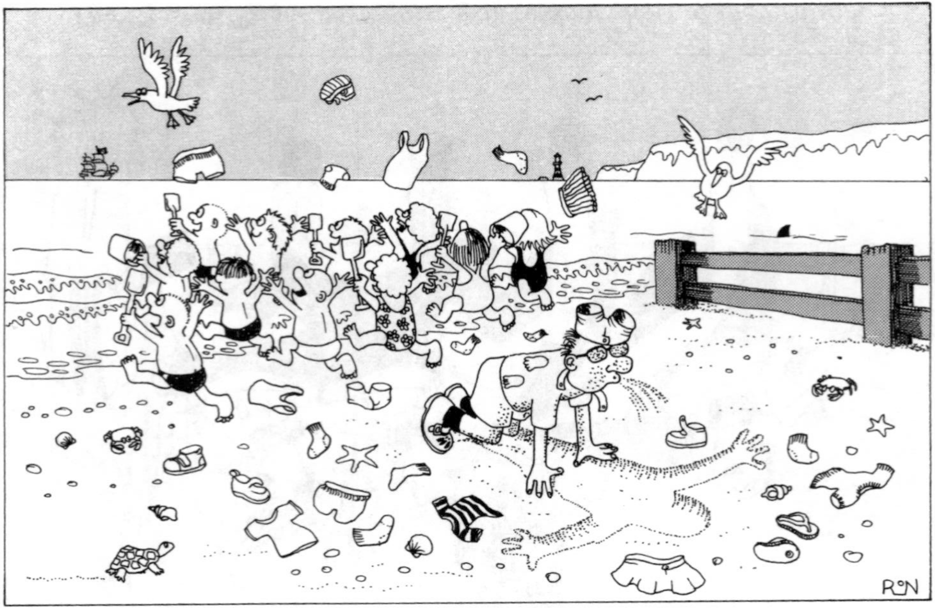
RON

The Sunday School outing was the high spot of Cecil's year.

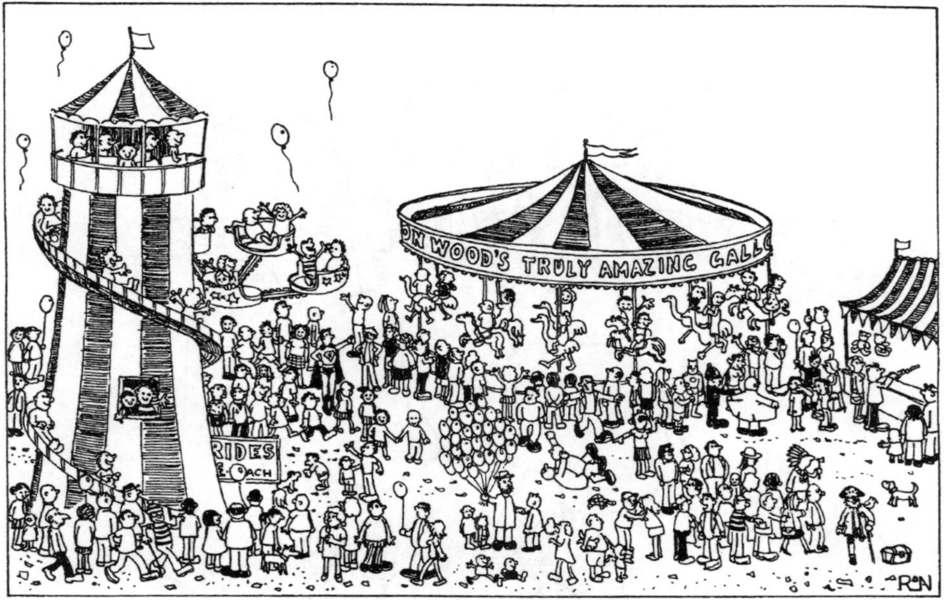
WOOD'S TRULY AMAZING
RIDES

Cedric felt very conspicuous in his dog-collar.

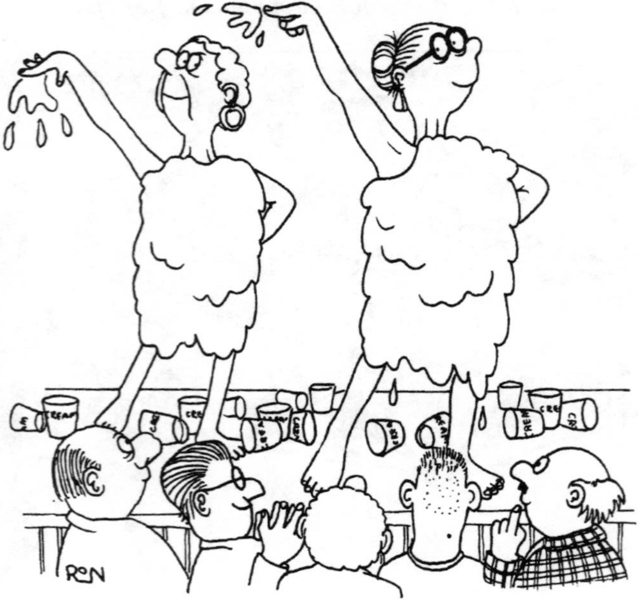
CREAM

The Mothers' Union raised funds with their ever-popular cream tease.

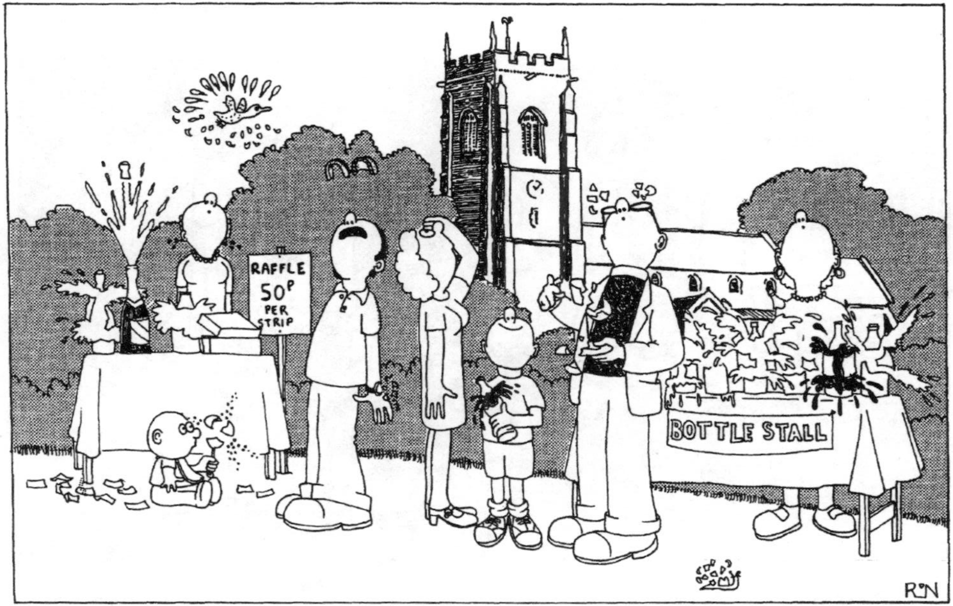
RAFFLE
50P
PER
STRIP
BOTTLE STALL
RN

The Church Garden Party ended with a display by the Red Arrows.

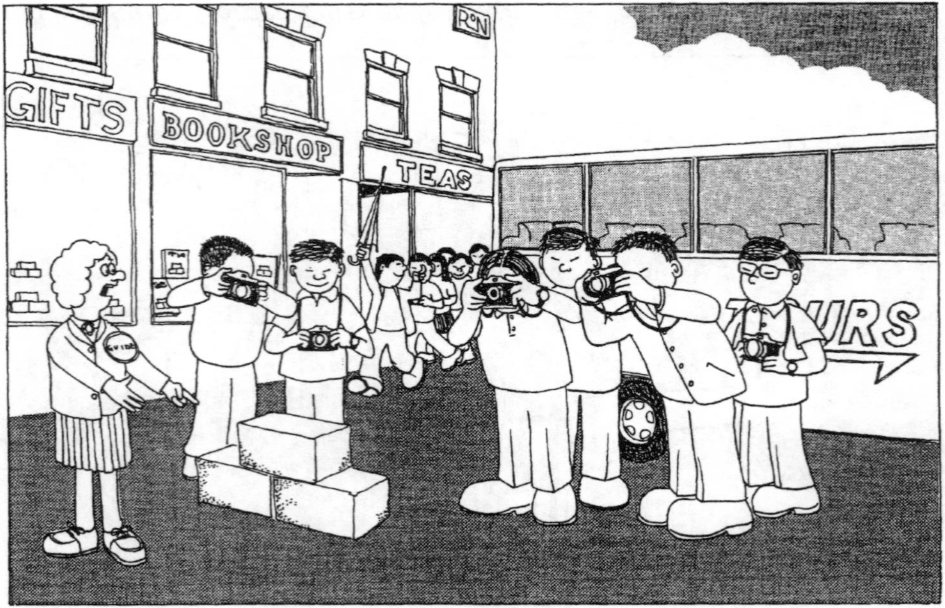
GIFTS
BOOKSHOP
TEAS
GUIDE

Begun in 1126, the Cathedral was still unfinished.

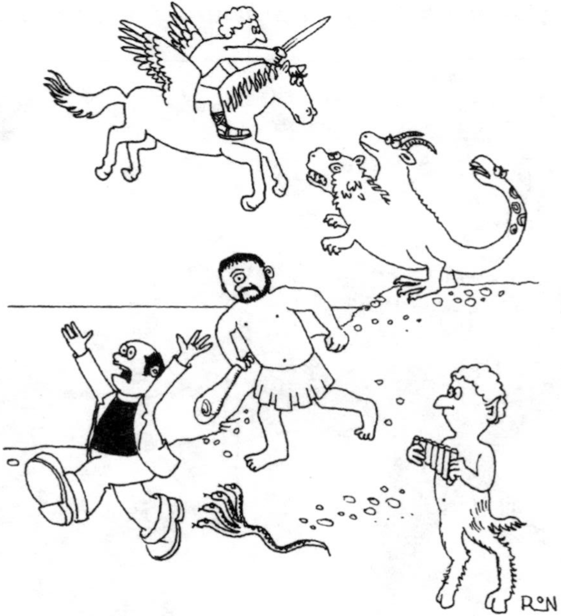
RON

Chaplaincy on a Greek island had looked good in the Church Times.

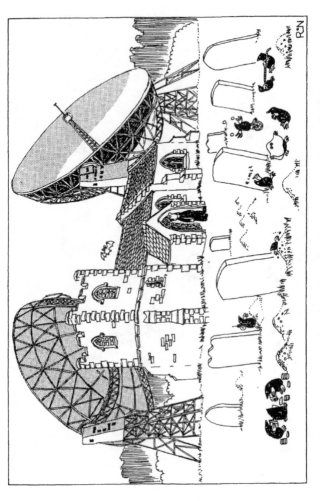

The search went on for intelligent life in Bishops Wibbling.

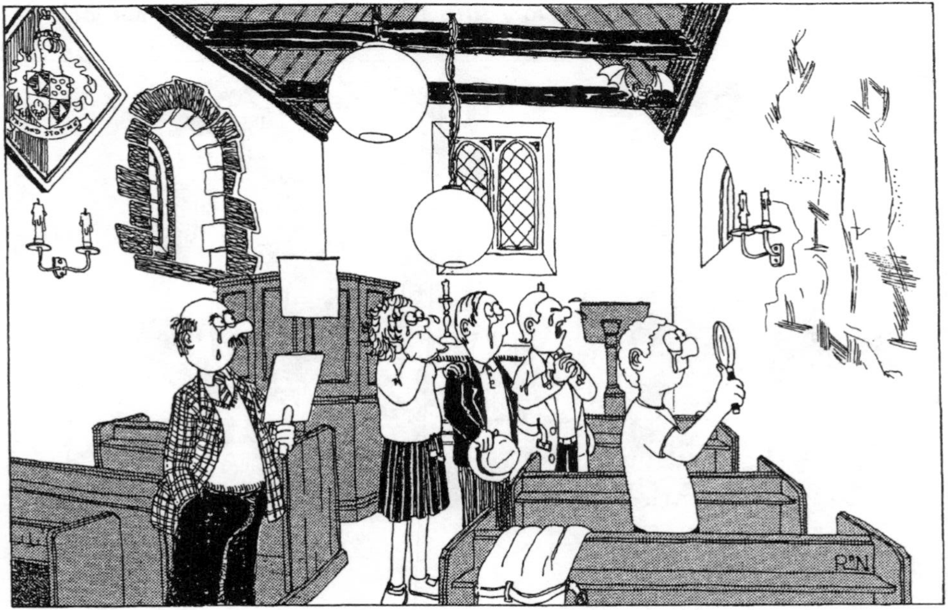

Ancient murals showed the feeding of 5,000, the raising of Lazarus, and England winning at cricket.

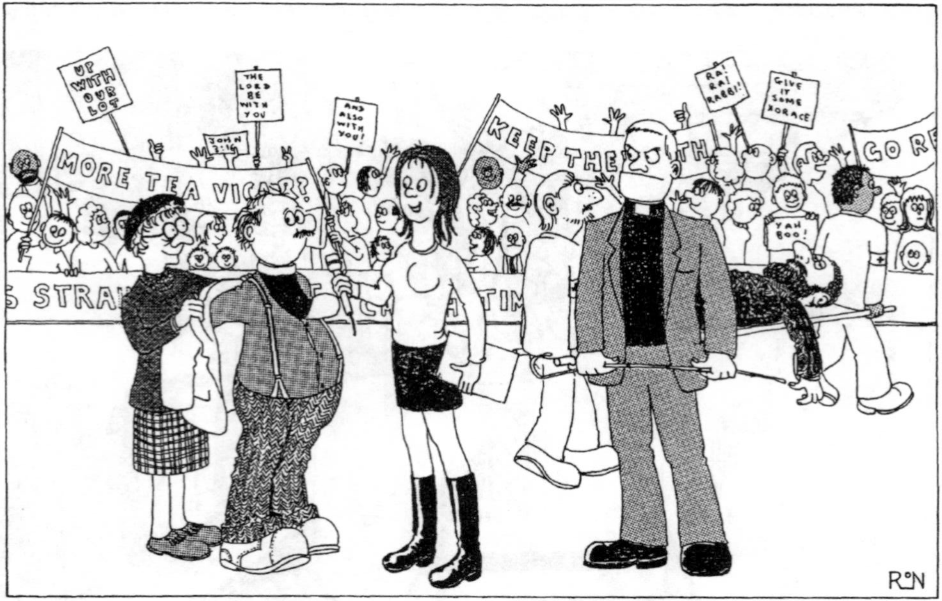
UP WITH OUR LOT
THE LORD BE WITH YOU
JOHN 3:16
AND ALSO WITH YOU!
MORE TEA VICAR?
KEEP THE
TH
RA! RA! RABBI!
GIVE IT SOME HORACE
YAH BOO!
GO R
RON

Victory over the Rabbi meant that Horace faced the Strict Baptist in the semi-final.

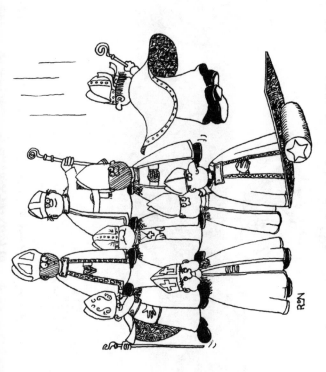

And then came the moment the whole conference had been working towards.

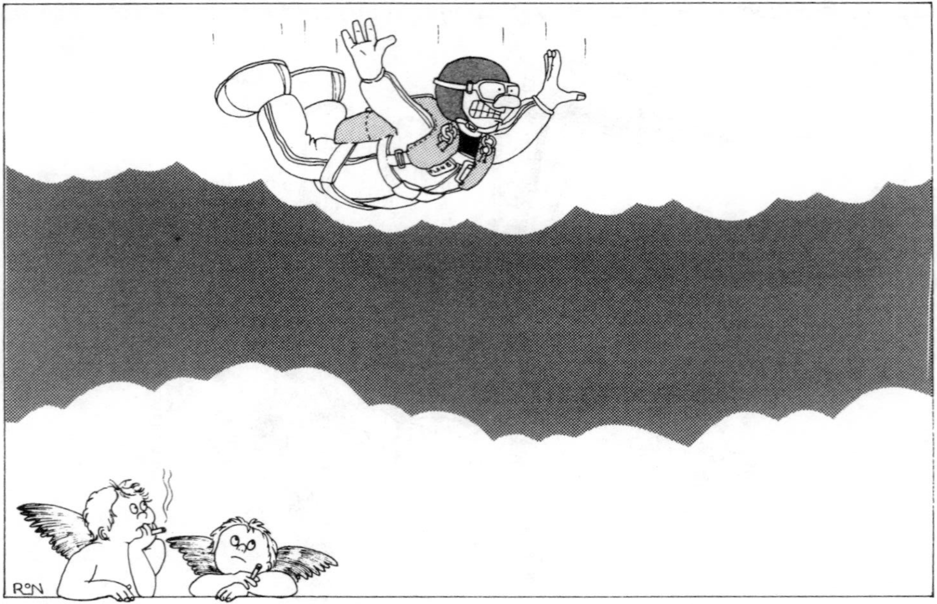
RON

On the way down, the Revd Eamonn Pules sang 'Nearer my God to theeeeeeeeeee ...'

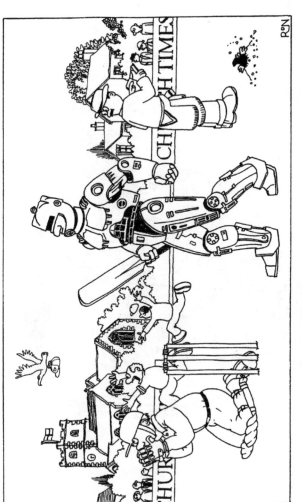

RoboVicar's preaching left a lot to be desired, but his batting average was impressive.

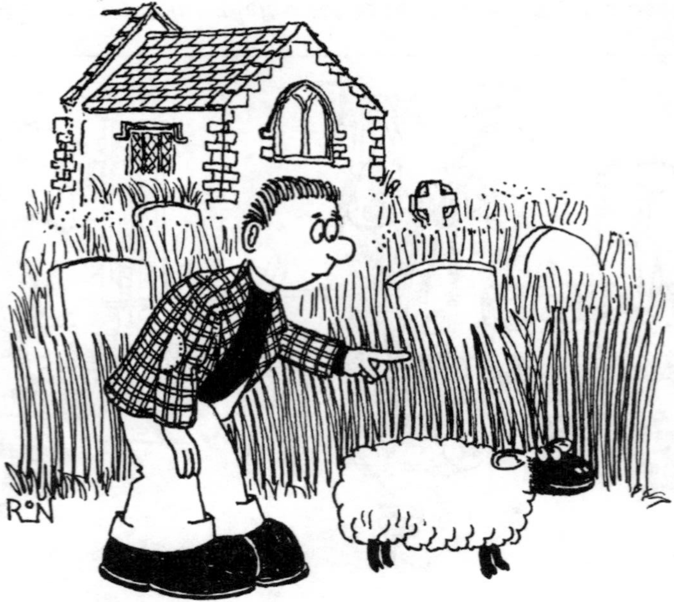
RON

The harvest was great, but the workers were few.

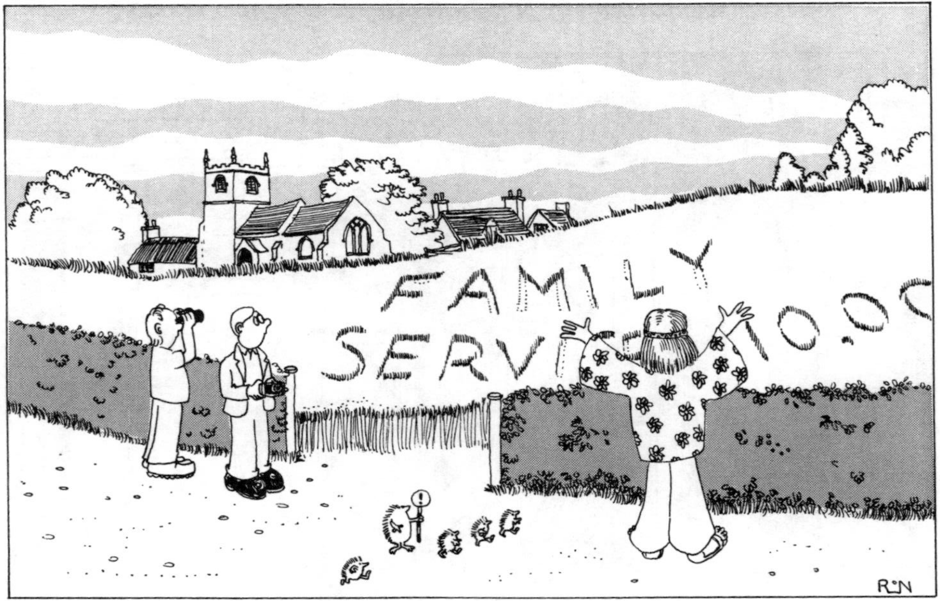
FAMILY
SERV 10.0

Some thought the crop circles had spiritual significance.

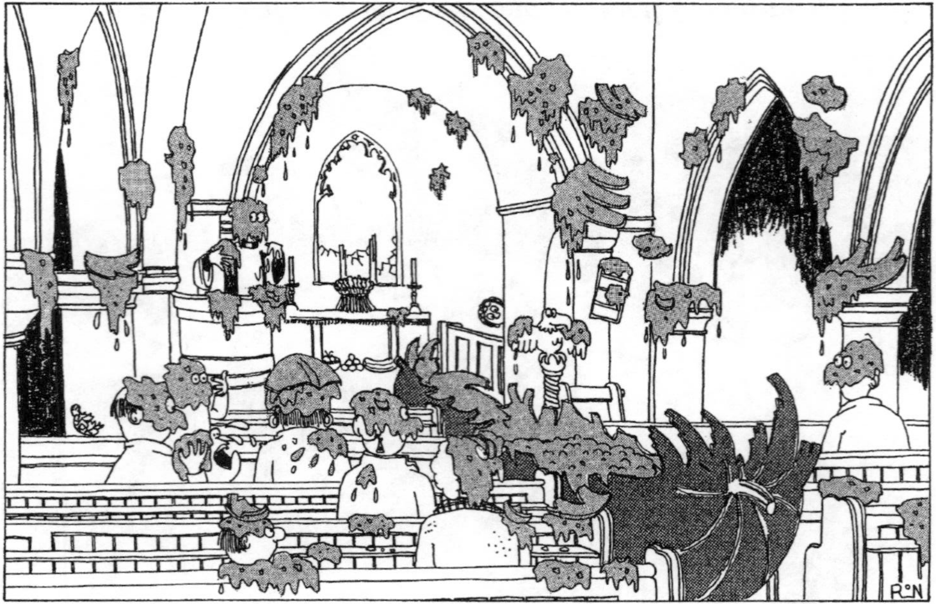

Nobody would ever forget the day the marrow exploded.

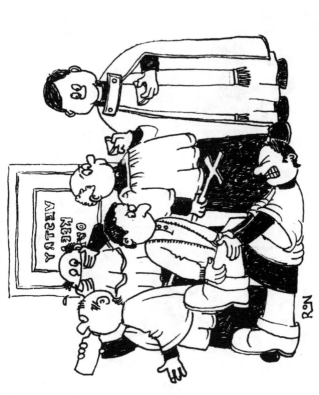

At half-time, the team came off for oranges and physiotherapy.

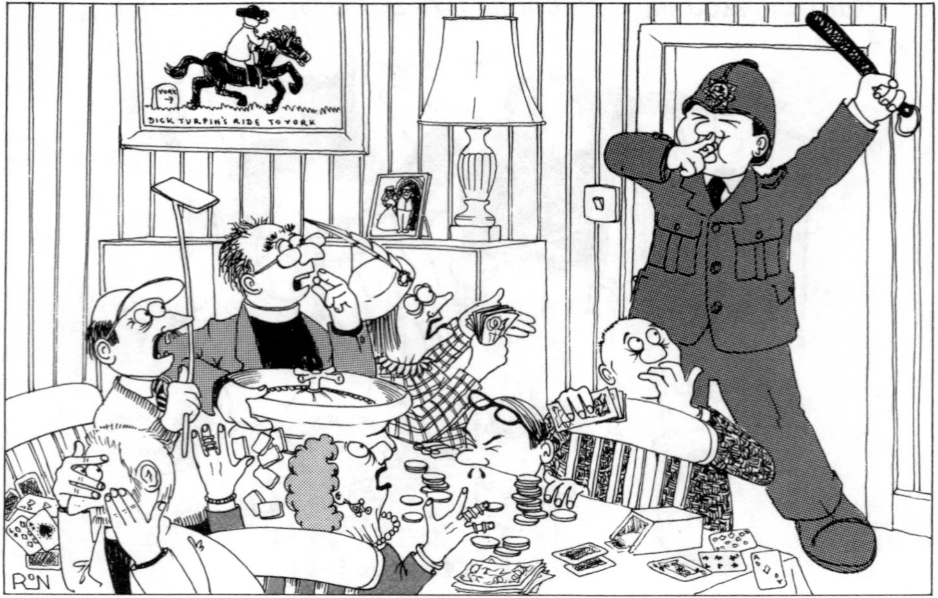
YORK
DICK TURPIN'S RIDE TO YORK
RON

The police interrupted some serious fund raising.

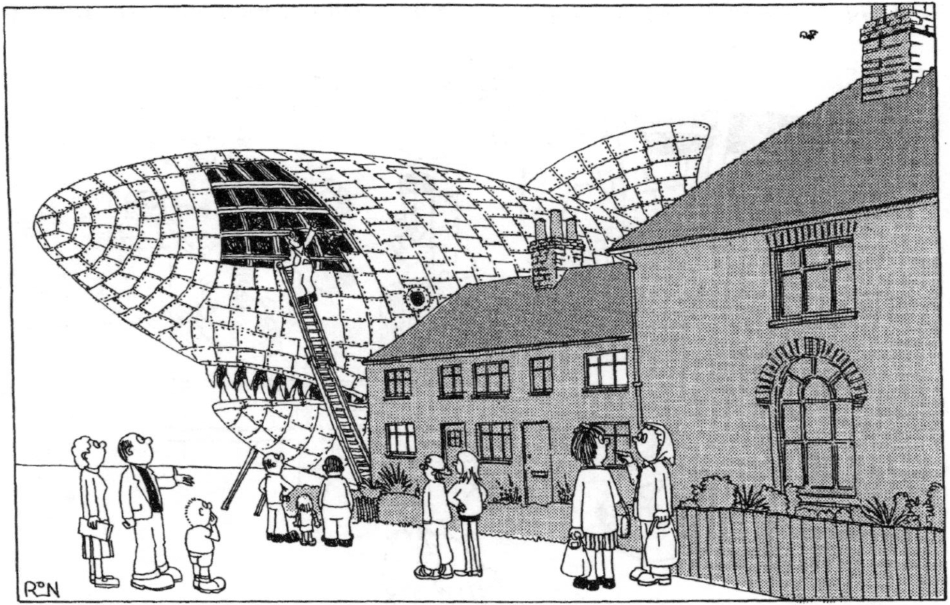
RON

The neighbours thought that if God had spoken to Neville, he'd not heard Him properly.

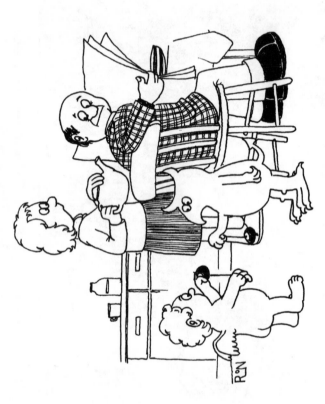

An epic struggle between good and evil took place in the vicarage kitchen.

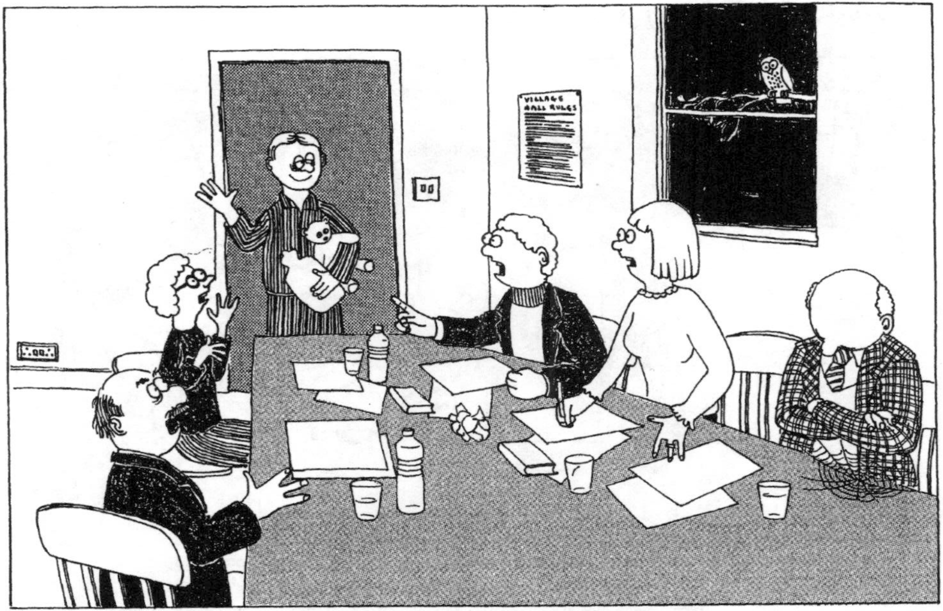
VILLAGE
HALL RULES

The Vicar's announcement he was retiring stunned the PCC.

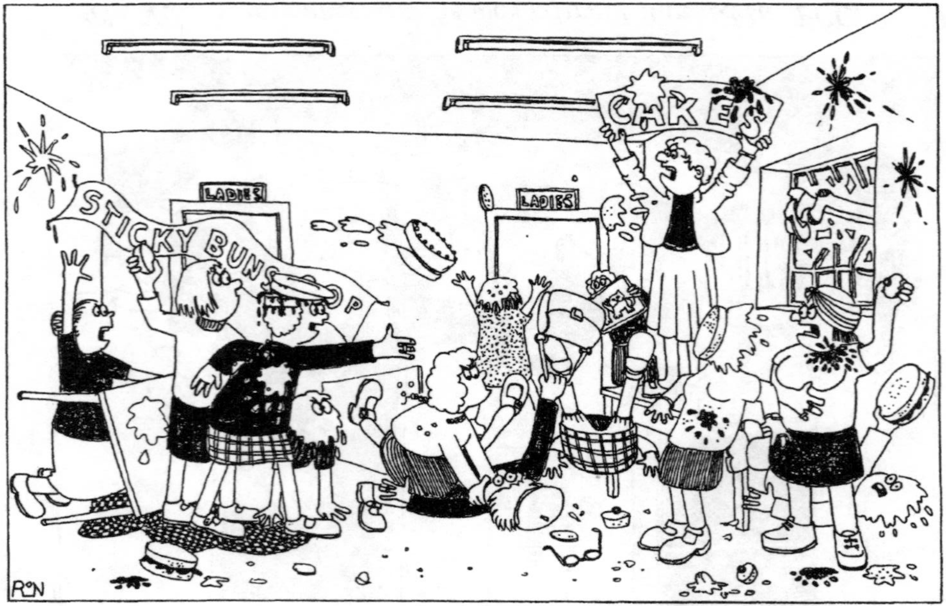
CAKES
LADIES
LADIES
STICKY BUNS
RON

The W.I. Sale of Work clashed with the Mothers' Union Winter Bazaar.

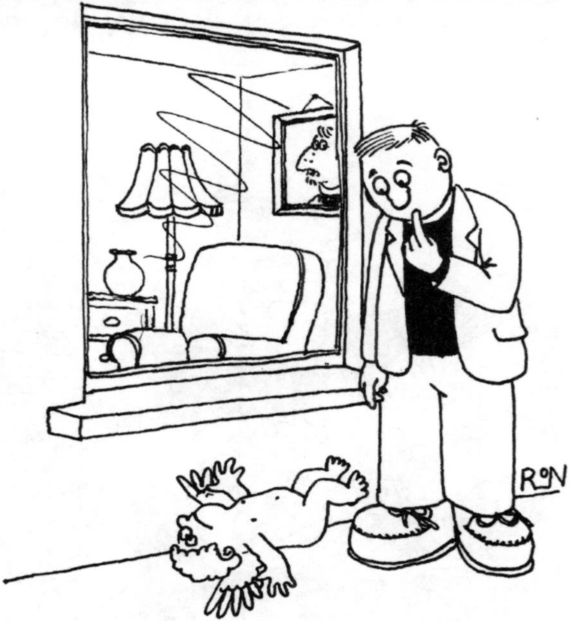
RON

The new windows at the vicarage proved an unexpected hazard.

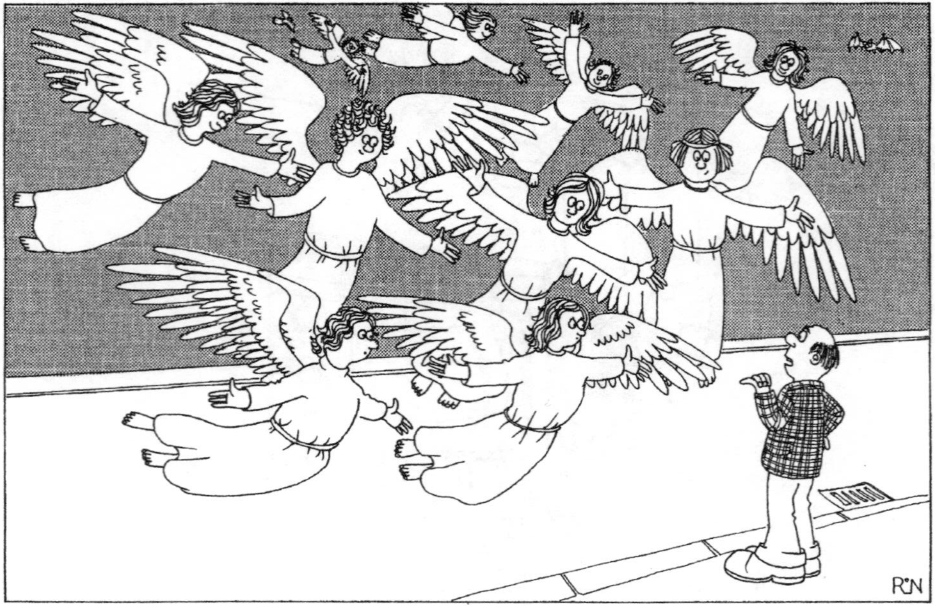
RN

'No,' said Mr Miles, 'the Robinson's are at number five.'

For a while, the argument seemed to favour 'The English Hymnal.'

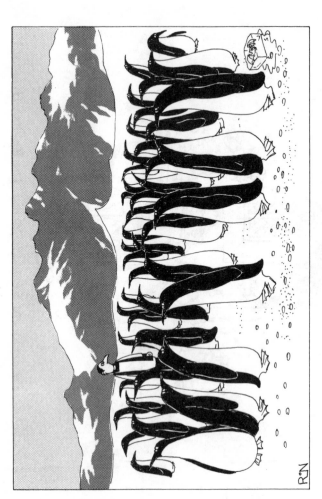

After a short while, they simply accepted Hugh as one of them.